# TIBETAN
## phrasebook

## Sandup Tsering

**Tibetan phrasebook**
  2nd edition

**Published by**
  **Lonely Planet Publications**
  Head Office: PO Box 617, Hawthorn, Vic 3122, Australia
  Branches:    155 Filbert St, Suite 251, Oakland, CA 94607, USA
               10 Barley Mow Passage, Chiswick, W4 4PH, UK
               71 bis rue du Cardinal Lemoine, 75005 Paris, France

**Printed by**
  Colorcraft Ltd, Hong Kong

**Cover Photograph**
  Prayer flags, detail (Chris Taylor)

**Published**
  June 1996

National Library of Australia Cataloguing in Publication Data

Tsering, Sandup, 1959-
  Tibetan phrasebook.

  2nd ed.
  Includes index.
  ISBN 0 86442 346 2.

  1. Tibetan language - Conversation and phrase books - English. I. Sandup
  Tsering, 1959-. II. Goldstein, Melvyn C. Tibet phrasebook. III. Title. IV.
  Title: Tibet phasebook (Series: Lonely Planet language survival kit).

495.483421

# Contents

**From the Publisher**

This edition was edited by Sally Steward and Nicola Daly. Louise Callan assisted with proofreading. Penelope Richardson designed and illustrated the book, and Simon Bracken designed the cover. Thanks to Rob Flynn for computer assistance, and many *changs* are due to all those involved in sticking down script.

**About the Authors**

Melvyn C Goldstein is the author of the first edition of the *Tibetan phrasebook*. He is a leading authority on the Tibetan language. He is also the author of several books on the language and country, including an excellent account of modern Tibet in *A History of Modern Tibet 1913-1951 – the demise of the lamaist state* (University of California Press, 1989).

Sandup Tsering, author of the second edition, is a linguist, translator and native speaker of Tibetan.

**This Edition**

This edition was written by Sandup Tsering. He has also supplied the computer-generated Tibetan script.

# Introduction

In Tibet it is not easy to get by with only English as the number of English speakers is relatively small, even in the capital, Lhasa. Once the world of villagers and nomads is entered, Chinese is also virtually nonexistent. This phrasebook aims to help travellers in Tibet converse and communicate with Tibetans and so enjoy their time in Tibet even more. As in any country, the locals will greatly appreciate your attempts to speak their language.

Tibetan is part of the Tibeto-Burman linguistic subgroup of the Sino-Tibetan language family. Of all the Asian languages, its closest relative is Burmese. Tibetan is spoken by more than six million people in Tibet and by many people in neighbouring countries such as India, Nepal and Bhutan.

Tibetan is characterised by many dialects, which may pose a problem for the traveller planning to visit different regions within Tibet. However, the dialect used in this book is the most widely understood dialect.

7

INTRODUCTION

Written Tibetan uses a script that was adapted from Sanskrit in 7 AD by Tibetan scholars who had been sent to India to study Sanskrit. Spellings have not been significantly revised since then which means that, due to changes in spoken Tibetan over the last 12 centuries, written and spoken Tibetan are very different.

This book includes both Tibetan script and a Romanised version of the script which will allow the traveller to pronounce Tibetan words and phrases.

## Getting Started

If you have trouble making yourself understood, just point to the Tibetan script on the right-hand side of the page. There are, however, a few basic words that would be useful to memorise and practise.

There is no equivalent for 'Hello' in Tibetan – it is common for Tibetans to ask a question such as 'How are you?' *(kayrang gusu debo yimbay?)*, or 'Where are you going?' *(kaba payga?)* . Sometimes the greeting *tashidelek* which literally means 'Good fortune' is used, however it is not considered equivalent to 'Hello'. 'Goodbye' is *kâliy shu* if you are leaving or *kâliy pay* if someone else is leaving. For more information on greetings see page 29. How to say 'Yes' and 'No' is on page 26. 'Thanks' is *tujaychay* and, if you're having trouble understanding someone, say *ha ko masong* ('I don't understand') or *kâliy kâliy sundâ* ('Say it slowly'). Other phrases to help you with language difficulties are on page 45.

# Pronunciation

The transliteration (Romanisation) system we have used in this book is designed to help you pronounce Tibetan sounds with ease. Like Chinese or Thai, tonal differences in Tibetan are used to convey meaning. However, unlike Chinese or Thai, they are not crucial and you will be understood without using them. For this reason tonal differences have not been included in this book.

To assist readers in correct pronunciation, a hyphen has been occasionally placed between syllables, particularly when two syllables end and begin with the same consonant or when there is a long or difficult combination of letters.

### Consonants
This section shows how to pronounce consonant sounds in Tibetan which are either not present in English, or are modified in some way.

| | |
|---|---|
| **k** | as in 'skip'. This sound is not breathy, so it can sound more like a 'g' than a 'k'.<br>*kang-ba*   leg |
| **kh** | a breathy 'k' like the 'k' in 'key'<br>*khang-ba*   house        *khong*   he/she |

9

| | | | |
|---|---|---|---|
| KA | KHA | GA | NGA |
| CA | CHA | JA | NYA |
| TA | THA | DA | NA |
| PA | PHA | BA | MA |
| TSA | TSHA | DZA | WA |
| ZHA | ZA | 'A | YA |
| RA | LA | SHA | SA |
| | HA | A | |

**khy**  like the 'cu' in 'cute'

    *khya*    to be cold    *khyu*    a herd

**gy**  like the 'gu' in 'regulate'

    *gyu!*    Go away!    *gyay*    eight

**ng**  as in 'sing'. This sound is easier to pronounce at the beginning of a word if you practise by saying 'singer' then repeating the word without the 'si' sound.

    *nga*    I    *ngay*    my

**ny**  like the 'ny' in 'canyon'

    *nya*    fish    *nyugu*    pen

| | |
|---|---|
| **t** | like the 't' in 'star'. This sound is not breathy so it can sound more like a 'd' than a 't'. |

    *teb*     book         *târiy*   today

**th**     a breathy 't' sound like the 't' in 'tent'

    *thowa*   hammer     *thama*  *cigarette*

**tsh**     like the 'ts' in 'Patsy'

    *tshay*   vegetables     *tsha*  salt

**dz**     like the 'dds' 'addsup'

    *dze*   tip-top

**p**     like the 'p' in 'priest'. This sound is not breathy so it can sound more like a 'b' than a 'p' to English speakers.

    *pu*   son         *pâju*  cow

**ph**     is a breathy 'p' sound like the 'p' in 'pat'

    *phama*   parents     *phagiy*  that

**lh**     is a breathy 'l' like the 'l h' in 'cool headed'

    *lha*   god         *lho*  south

**thr**     a sound that is similar to the 'tr' in 'triumph', with the 'r' slightly rolled

    *thro*   wheat

**dr**     a sound similar to the 'dr' in 'dragon', with the 'r' slightly rolled

    *driy*   female yak

PRONUNCIATION

## *Vowels*

**a**  like the 'a' in 'father'
  *nga*  I  *sa*  earth

**i**  as in 'it'
  *rimba*  price

**iy**  as in 'see'
  *diy*  this

**â**  a short sound like the 'a' in 'alone'
  *lâb*  say

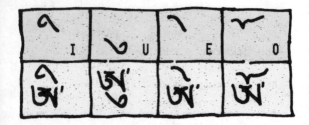

**o**  as in 'so' or 'dough'
  *mo*  she

**aw**  as in the British pronunciation of 'paw'
  *gaw*  want/need  *thowa*  hammer

**u**  similar to the 'oo' sound in 'glue'
  *su*  who  *gu*  nine

PRONUNCIATION

**e**    as in 'met'
    *me*    fire

**ay**    as in 'say'
    *tshay*    vegetables    *pay*    wool

**ö**    like the 'er' in 'her' pronounced with pursed lips
    *kö*    his    *pö*    Tibet

**ü**    like the 'ew' in 'crew'
    *sü*    whose    *ngü*    money/silver

## Nasalised Vowels

Nasalised vowels are indicated in the transliteration by an 'n', 'm' or 'ng' following a vowel. To achieve this sound, say the vowel pushing the air through the nose and mouth rather than just the mouth. For example in the word *langsha,* 'beef', the 'a' is nasalised because it is followed by 'ng'.

# Grammar

Tibetan grammar follows some basic rules, with few exceptions. This chapter will help you understand the phrases you'll be using, and give you the basics for stringing your own sentences together.

## Sentence Structure

Tibetan sentences generally follow the pattern: subject-object-verb. So the English sentence 'I saw the dog' becomes 'I the dog saw' in Tibetan.

I like rice.            *nga dray gawpo yö*
                        (lit: I rice like)
I need a map.           *nga sapta chig gaw*
                        (lit: I map one need )

## Articles
### Definite Article – 'the'

There is no exact equivalent of 'the' in Tibetan. However, the words 'this', 'that', 'these' and 'those' (demonstrative adjectives) are used in a similar way.

| | | | |
|---|---|---|---|
| this | *diy* | that | *phâgiy* |
| these | *dintso* | those | *phântso* |

The yak is black.     *yak diy nâg-bo ray*
(lit: yak this black is)

The rooms are dirty.     *nyekhang dintso tsogba ray*
(lit: room these dirty is)

### Indefinite Article – a/an

This is expressed in Tibetan by the use of the numeral 'one' which is *chig*.

a yak     *yak chig*
(lit: yak one)

a book     *teb chig*
(lit: book one)

## Nouns
### Plurals

Tibetan nouns do not change form in the plural. Plurality is expressed in one of three ways.

- A plural demonstrative adjective ('these' *dintso* or 'those' *phântso*) may be used to indicate plural:

   The bicycles are here.     *kâng-gâriy dintso day du*
   (lit: bicycle these here are)

GRAMMAR

- Plural words (eg. 'many' *mâng-po*, 'a few' *nyun-nyun*, etc.)
  or numerals may also be used to indicate plurality:

| | |
|---|---|
| There are many mountains in Tibet. | *pölâ riy mâng-po yawray* (lit: Tibet in mountain many are) |

- A third way to show plurality is through context, or through the absence of the indefinite article *chig* (a/an/one):

| | |
|---|---|
| There are yaks in Tibet. | *pö-la yak yawray* (lit: Tibet in yak are) |

## Adjectives

Adjectives come after the nouns they describe.

| | |
|---|---|
| red suitcase | *dogthray ma-bo* (lit: suitcase red) |
| dirty room | *nyekhang tsogba* (lit: room dirty) |

### Common Adjectives

| | |
|---|---|
| good | *yagpo* |
| bad | *dukcha* |
| big | *chembo* |
| small | *chunchun* |
| happy | *kiybu* |
| many | *mâng-po* |
| few | *nyun-nyun* |
| cold | *trang-mo* |
| hot | *tshabo* |

| big horse | *ta chembo* |
|---|---|
| | (lit: horse big) |
| This is good. | *diy yagpo du* |
| | (lit: this good is) |
| The food was very delicious. | *kala shimpo shedra du* |
| | (lit: food very delicious is) |

## Comparatives – 'er'

If you want to say something is, for example, 'bigger' or 'better', take the first syllable of the adjective (the adjective stem), and add either *pa* or *wa* onto the end. Sometimes the adjective stem changes its form when *pa* or *wa* is added (eg. 'bigger' in examples below, *chemb* becomes *chay*). Here are a few of the more common words with the appropriate endings added.

GRAMMAR

| good | *yagpo* | better | *yak-pa* |
|---|---|---|---|
| big | *chembo* | bigger | *chay-wa* |
| many | *mâng-po* | more | *mâng-wa* |
| bad | *dukcha* | worse | *duk-pa* |

If you want to compare things in a sentence, use the word *lay* after the item being compared. The word *lay* roughly translates as 'than'. For example, if you want to say 'My horse is bigger than your horse', put the *lay* after 'your horse'.

| My horse is bigger than your horse. | *ngay ta kayrâng-ki ta lay chay-wa yawray* |
|---|---|
| | (lit: my horse your horse than bigger is) |

**Superlatives – 'est'**
Superlatives work exactly the same way as comparatives, except the ending is different. When you want to say something is, for example, 'the best' or 'biggest', add *shö* to the first syllable of the adjective.

| good | *yagpo* | best | *yag-shö* |
|------|---------|------|-----------|
| big | *chembo* | biggest | *chay-shö* |
| many | *mâng-po* | most | *mâng-shö* |
| bad | *dukcha* | worst | *duk-shö* |

## *Pronouns*
**Personal Pronouns**

| I/me | *nga* | we/us | *ngânts* |
|------|-------|-------|----------|
| you (sg) | *kayrang* | you (pl) | *kayrântso* |
| he/him | *kho* | they/them | *khontso* |
| she/her | *mo* | | |
| he/she (polite) | *khong* | | |

Pronouns are the same whether the pronoun is acting as a subject (eg. 'I'), or an object (eg. 'me').

I am a student.  *nga lob-trug yin*
(lit: I student am)

He gave a book to her.  *khö mo-la teb chig nâng-song*
(lit: he her to book one gave)

GRAMMAR

**Possessive Pronouns**

| | | | |
|---|---|---|---|
| my/mine | *ngay* | our/ours | *ngântsö* |
| your(s) | *kayrâng-giy* | your(s) | *kayrâng-tsö* |
| his | *khö* | their(s) | *khong-tsö* |
| her/hers | *mö* | | |
| his/her (polite) | *khong-giy* | | |

| | |
|---|---|
| her book | *mö tep* |
| his film | *khö phingsho* |
| That is mine. | *phagiy ngay ray* |
| | (lit: that mine is) |

## *Possession*
### Have/Has

Possession is expressed in Tibetan by adding *la* (which means 'to' or 'at') to the end of the subject, and using the verb *du* or *yö* ('to be') at the end of the sentence. Thus, 'He has a book' is expressed as 'to (at) him there is a book'.

| | |
|---|---|
| He has a book. | *kaw la tep chig du* |
| | (*kho la* is pronounced *kaw la*) |
| They have a camera. | *kontso la parchay chig du* |
| | (lit: they at camera one is) |

GRAMMAR

### Verbs

There are two classes of Tibetan verbs. One class contains verbs which the subject controls, referred to here as 'intentional verbs'. For example, 'to eat', or 'to kick'. The other class of verbs are those which represent actions or feelings which the subject does not have direct control over. Examples of these are 'to feel sick', or 'to feel sad'. These will be called 'unintentional verbs'. Some verbs can have both an 'intentional' and an 'unintentional' form. For example, in Tibetan the verb 'to sleep' has an 'intentional' form, meaning the person went to sleep of their own volition, and an 'unintentional' form meaning the person fell asleep without wanting to. These two classes of verbs have different endings depending on when the action is done (present, past, or future), and who the action is done by (me, you, or he/she).

Another feature of Tibetan verbs is that they change in form for past and present/future. For example, for the verb 'to eat' *sa*, becomes *say* in the past tense and *sâ* in the present/future tense.

**Intentional Verbs**

|  | Present | Past | Future |
|---|---|---|---|
| **I/we** | verb + *giyö* | verb + *bâyin* | verb + *giyin* |
| **you/he/she/they** | verb + *giydu* | verb + *bâray* | verb + *giray* |

| | |
|---|---|
| She ate food. | *mö kala say-**bâray*** |
| | (lit: she food eat past) |
| They will eat food. | *khontso kala sâ-**giray*** |
| | (lit: They food eat future) |

The subject of an intentional verb changes from *nga*, which is 'I' to *ngay* ('by me') in the past and present.

| | |
|---|---|
| I eat food. | *ngay kala sa-**giyö*** |
| | (lit: by me food eat present ) |

**Unintentional Verbs**

|  | Present | Past | Future |
|---|---|---|---|
| **I/we** | verb + *giydu* | verb + *chung* | verb + *giray* |
| **you/he/she they** | verb + *giydu* | verb + *song* | verb + *girayu* |

For any sentences using an unintentional verb such as 'sleep' or 'sick', add *giray* to the end of the verb for future tense, and *giydu* to the end of the verb for present tense.

| I/They will become sick. | *nga/khontso na-**giyray*** |
| | (lit: I/they sick future) |
| I/They am/are sick. | *nga/khontso na-**giydu*** |
| | (lit: I/they sick past) |

For the past tense add the ending *chung* to the end of the verb when the sentence begins with 'I' or 'we':

| I became sick. | *nga na-**chung*** |
| | (lit: I sick past) |

When the sentence begins with 'you', 'he/she' or 'they' add the ending *song* to the verb:

| They became sick. | *khontso na-**song*** |
| | (lit: they sick past) |

GRAMMAR

## To Be

One of the most important differences between English and Tibetan grammar is in the verb 'to be' (is/are). English uses one word (is/are) to express both 'existence' – 'the book is (exists) here' – and 'having a quality' – 'the book is red'. Tibetan, on the other hand, uses three different verbs.

- The verb *du*, 'to be', is used to express location, possession and feeling. The use of this verb also implies that the knowledge in the sentence was gained first-hand.

| The forest is here. | *shing-na day du* |
| | (lit: forest here is) |
| He has a backpack. | *kho-la gyâb-pay chig du* |
| | (lit: to him backpack one is) |

The verb *du* becomes *yö* when it is used with 'I' or 'we'.

| I like fish. | *nga nya la gâbo yö*<br>(lit: I fish like is) |

- To express a quality or state, the verb *ray* is used.

| This room is dirty. | *nyekhang diy tsogba ray*<br>(lit: room this dirty is) |
| He is Dorje. | *kho dorje ray*<br>(lit: he Dorje is) |
| The pen is red. | *nyugu diy ma-bo ray*<br>(lit: pen this red is) |

The verb *ray* becomes *yin* when it is used with 'I' or 'we'.

| I am a teacher. | *nga gegen yin*<br>(lit: I teacher am) |

- The verb *yawray* is used to express facts which are general or common knowledge.

| There are yaks in Tibet. | *pö-lâ yak yawray*<br>(lit: Tibet in yak are) |
| He is a good person. | *khong mi yagpo yawray*<br>(lit: he person good is) |

## Questions

There are two main ways to form questions in Tibetan. One is to change the verb at the end of the sentence. The other is to use question words such as 'who', 'what', 'which', etc.

GRAMMAR

## Changing the Verb

To make a question from a sentence using one of the three forms of the verb 'to be', the endings change in the following ways:

- *du* becomes *dugay*. The stress in *dugay* is on the *gay*.
  Are there hot springs here?　*day chutshen dugay?*
  　　　　　　　　　　　　　(lit: here hot springs are?)

- *ray* changes to *rebay*. The stress in the word *rebay* is on the *bay*.
  Is this a guesthouse?　　*diy drönkâng rebay?*
  　　　　　　　　　　　　(lit: this guesthouse is?)

- *yawray* changes to *yawrebay*. The stress in the word *rebay* is on the *bay*.
  Are yaks big?　　　　　*yak chembo yawrebay?*
  　　　　　　　　　　　(lit: yak big are?)

- For the verb 'to want', *gaw* changes to *gawbay*.
  Do you want tea?　　　*kayrâng cha gawbay?*
  　　　　　　　　　　　(lit: you tea want?)

## Question Words

Another way to create a question is to use a question word.

| what | *kâray* | What is this? |
| | | *diy kâray ray?* |
| | | What did you eat? |
| | | *kayrâng kâray saybâyin?* |
| who | *su* | Who is this? |
| | | *diy su ray?* |

GRAMMAR

| where | **kâba** (stress on *ba*) | Where is the hospital? *men-khâng kâba du?* |
| when | **kâdü** | When did you eat? *kayrâng kala kâdü say-bâyin?* |
| whose | **sü** | Whose is this? *diy sü ray?* |
| how many/ much | **kâtsö** | How many rooms are there? *nyekhâng kâtsö du?* |
| why | **kâray-chaynay** | Why did you go? *kayrâng kâray chaynay chin-bâyin?* |

GRAMMAR

## Negatives

To make a verb negative in Tibetan, just add either *ma* or *min* to the beginning or middle of the verb. For example, the three forms of the verb 'to be' change in the following way:

| | | | |
|---|---|---|---|
| *ray* | (is/are) | ⟶ | *ma-ray* (not is/are) |
| *du* | (is/are) | ⟶ | *min-du* (not is/are) |
| *yawray* | (is/are) | ⟶ | *yawma-ray* (not is/are) |

This is not a restaurant.    *diy sakhâng mâray*
(lit: this restaurant not is)

There are no birds here.    *day cha mindu*
(lit: here bird not are)

## Conveying Yes & No

To say 'Yes' and 'No' in Tibetan, the affirmative and negative of the verbs 'to be' (*du*, *ray* and *yawray*) are used.

| Question Form of Verb | Yes | No |
|---|---|---|
| *rebay* ('to be') | *ray* | *maray* |
| *dugay* ('to be') | *du* | *mindu* |
| *yawrebay* ('to be') | *yawray* | *yaw-mâray* |
| *gawbay* ('to want') | *gaw* | *mögaw* |

Normally one answers according to the verb used in the question. For example, if you are asked 'Is Tibet nice/pleasant?' (*pö kibo dugay?*) the affirmative answer would be *du* and the negative would be *mindu*. If the question used *yawrebay*, the response for 'Yes' and 'No' would be different, for example:

| | |
|---|---|
| Are yaks big? | *yak chembo yawrebay?* |
| Yes. | *yawray* |
| No. | *yaw-mâray* |

Similarly, if the person asking the question used a different verb such as 'to want/need' (*gaw*), the equivalent for 'Yes' and 'No' would be different. For example:

| | |
|---|---|
| Do you want tea? | *kayrang cha gawbay* |
| Yes. | *gaw* |
| No. | *mögaw* |

## Want, Need, Must

In Tibetan one word, *gaw*, is used to mean 'want', 'need' and 'must'.

| | |
|---|---|
| I want tea. | *nga cha gaw* |
| | (lit: I tea want) |

GRAMMAR

| I need two beds. | *nga nyethri nyi gaw* |
| | (lit: I bed two need) |
| I must see the forest. | *nga shing-na mig ta-gaw yö* |
| | (lit: I forest eye see must) |

To make a question, use a question word, such as 'how much' *kâtsö*.

| How much money do you want? | *kayrângla ngü kâtsö gaw?* |
| | (lit: you money how much want?) |

To make a negative, add *mö* to the beginning of *gaw*.

| I don't want this. | *nga-la diy mögaw* |
| | (lit: I this don't want) |

## Prepositions

Prepositions come after the noun.

| In front of the house. | *khâng-ba dün-la* |
| | (lit: house in front of) |

| above | *gâng-la* |
| across from | *pha-chogla* |
| adjacent (next) to | *triy-la* |
| around | *nyeko-la* |
| at | *la* |
| behind | *gyâb-la/jay-la* |
| beside | *triy-la* |
| from | *nay* |
| in | *nâng-la* |
| in front of | *dün-la* |

| of | *kiy/giy/yi* |
| on | *gâng-la* |
| opposite | *katrö-la/togchog-la* |
| under | *ohg-la* |
| with | *nyâm-du* |

## Conjunctions

| and/because | *tâng/kâyin-sayna* |
| but | *yin-nay* |
| or | *yâng-na* |
| since | *tsâng/nay* |
| so (therefore) | *te-dah song-tsâng* |
| so that (in order to) | *tondâg-la/chay-du* |
| then | *de-nay/de-du* |

# Greetings & Civilities

### *Greetings*

In Tibetan there is no equivalent for 'Hello'. Traditionally, if Tibetans gave a greeting they asked where a person was going. Today in India and Nepal some Tibetans have begun using the phrase *tashidelek*, which literally means 'Good fortune'. While this is sometimes used in Lhasa, it would not normally be understood as an equivalent to 'Hello'. In Tibet people simply get on with a question or statement without first saying anything equivalent to 'Hello'.

Other phrases which are used when greeting people are:

Good morning.
   *nga-to delek*        ཞུ་རྟོ་བདེ་ལེགས།
How are you?
   *kayrang kusu debo yimbay?*  ཁྱེད་རང་སྐུ་གཟུགས་བདེ་པོ་ཡིན་པས།
I'm fine.
   *nga debo yin*        ང་བདེ་པོ་ཡིན།

It's useful to note that when calling on Tibetans at their house, one way of attracting attention (there are no doorbells) is to call

out *ulay, ulay*. Those inside, if they know you, will then invite
you in by probably saying *ya pay* ('Come in').

## Goodbye

Although Tibetans have no word for 'Hello', they do have two
terms for 'Goodbye' and they use both. One term, *kâliy shu*, is
said by the person leaving to the person staying. It literally means
'Stay slowly'. The other term, *kâliy pay*, is said by the person
staying to the person going. It literally means 'Go slowly'. The
following phrases may also be useful when saying 'Goodbye'.

It's time to go.
    *ta do-ran-sha*                ད་འགྲོ་རན་ཤག
We had a good time.
    *nga-tso kyipo chung*          ང་ཚོ་སྐྱིད་པོ་བྱུང་།
Good night.
    *simja nâng-gaw*               གཟིམ་འཇགས་གནང་དགོས།

See you tomorrow.
    *sânyi jay-yong*               སང་ཉིན་མཇལ་ཡོང་།
See you later.
    *jema jay-yong*                རྗེས་མ་མཇལ་ཡོང་།
Come again soon.
    *yâng-kya pheb-ro-ah*          ཡང་སྐྱར་ཕེབས་རོགས་ཨ།

## Civilities

The word for 'Please' in Tibetan is *kuchi* (inf) or *tujay-sig*. However, this word is only used when the request which follows is quite
desperate. For example, 'Please help me' is *kuchi, nga-la rog nang
dang*. There are a number of polite expressions for situations where
English speakers would use 'Please' or 'Thank you'.

(Please) come in.
*ya pay* ཡར་ཕེབས།

(Please) sit down.
*shu-denja* བཞུགས་གདན་འཇགས།

Thanks.
*tujay-chay* ཐུགས་རྗེ་ཆེ།

Thank you very much.
*tujay shita-chay* ཐུགས་རྗེ་ཞེ་དྲག་ཆེ།

Thank you for your hospitality.
*nay-len yakpo jepa tujay-chay* སྙེ་ལེན་ཡག་པོ་བྱེད་པ་ཐུགས་རྗེ་ཆེ།

Thank you for your help.
*rog nâng-wa tujay-chay* རོགས་གནང་བ་ཐུགས་རྗེ་ཆེ།

Not at all/Don't mention it.
*shu-goyak yaw maray* ཞུ་དགོས་ཡག་ཡོད་མ་རེད།

## Requests

I'd like to ask you a favour.
*ngay kayrâng-la raykul-chig shuyâk yaw* ངས་ཁྱེད་རང་ལ་རེ་སྐུལ་གཅིག་ཞུ་ཡག་ཡོད།

May I ask you a question?
*ngay kayrâng-la kayja-chig tina digiy rebay?* ངས་ཁྱེད་རང་ལ་སྐད་ཆ་གཅིག་འདྲི་ན་འགྲིག་གི་རེད་པས།

Please help me if you can.
*nga-la rog-chig nang thup-na nâng rog* ང་ལ་རོགས་གཅིག་གནང་ཐུབ་ན་གནང་རོགས།

(Please) could you repeat that?
*yâng-kya sung-ro nâng?* ཡང་སྐྱར་གསུང་རོགས་གནང་།

(Please) show me that.
*nga-la tön nâng tâng* ང་ལ་སྟོན་གནང་གནང་།

Will you pass it to me please?
   *nga-la shu-rog nang* ཌ་ལ་བཤུགས་རོགས་གནང་

Can I take ... now?
   *ta ... kye-na digiy rebay?* ད་ — བཞེར་ན་འགྲིག་གི་རེད་པས།

May I go now?
   *ta tona digiy rebay?* ད་ — འགྲོ་ན་འགྲིག་གི་རེད་པས།

Please don't forget!
   *(kuchi) majay-ro nang!* (སྐུ་སྱི་)མ་བརྗེད་རོགས་གནང་

What is the name of this?
   *diy minglâ, karay ray?* འདིའི་མིང་ལ་ག་རེ་རེད།

Go away!
   *pa gyu!* ཕར་རྒྱུགས།

Be quiet!
   *kaga shu!* ཁ་རྒ་བཞུགས།

## Apologies

I'm sorry/Pardon me.
   *gawn-da* དགོངས་དག

It's my fault.
   *ngay nor-tül ray* ངའི་ནོར་འཁྲུལ་རེད།

It doesn't matter.
   *kay nâng-gi maray* གར་ཡང་གནང་གི་མ་རེད།

Don't mention it.
   *sung goyak yaw maray* གསུངས་དགོས་ལགས་ཡོད་མ་རེད།

Sorry? What did you say?
   *kâng sung-pa, kuchi yâng-kya* གང་གསུངས་པ། སྐུ་མཆིན་ཡང་སྐྱར་གསུངས་རོགས་
   *sung-ro nâng?*

## Honorific Language

Honorific language consists of a range of special vocabulary which is used to show respect to another person. It is used mainly in central Tibet, particularly in the capital Lhasa where people use it so much that they even have honorific names for their possessions such as household goods and pets. While its usage is important in Tibetan society, foreigners aren't expected to know how to use it. However, it is recommended that you address people in a polite way. This is usually done by just adding *la* after names or titles, for example, *Tenzin* is *Tenzin la* and *ama* ('mother') is *ama la*.

## Names

Usually families obtain names for their children from Lamas (spiritual guides), before or soon after the birth. They are given two names of which the first is the name of the Lama. This becomes the child's given name. Sometimes, however, abbreviations or combinations of both first and second names are used. Tibetans also have a family name or surname which is taken from the name of their ancestral home, but it isn't commonly used. Married couples share

the family name of the household that they live in. So, for example, if the husband joins his wife's household, he takes his wife's family name.

In Tibetan, there are not specific boys' and girls' names. It is the combination of the two given names which indicates gender, not the name itself. For instance, the name *Tenzin* when combined with the name *Dorje* is considered masculine, however when combined with the name *Dolma*, it is considered feminine.

### Some Common Given Names & Their Meanings

| | |
|---|---|
| *Dorje* | 'thunderbolt' or 'sceptre' |
| *Dhondup* | 'wish fulfillment' |
| *Dolma* | Goddess of Compassion |
| *Gonpo* | 'protector' |
| *Gyatso* | 'ocean' |
| *Lobsang* | 'kindheart' |
| *Nyima* | 'sun' |
| *Norbu* | 'jewel' |
| *Sherap* | 'wisdom' |
| *Tenzin* | 'holder of Buddha's teaching' |

## Attracting Someone's Attention

To attract a stranger's attention, Tibetans do not say 'Excuse me' but rather call out to the person using one of a series of kinship terms that vary according to the age and sex of the other person. The standard term for an adult male about one's own age is *chola* (literally, 'elder brother' or male of the same generation). It is equivalent to '(Hey) Mister'. Thus, you might say to a man on the street who you don't know but is about your age: *chola, gomba kaba du?* ('Hey Mister, where is the monastery?'). If the person you are talking to is a young boy, the term used is *pu* (literally, 'son'). For an elderly man the term is *pola* (literally, 'grandfather'), and for an older, but not elderly man, the term *pala* (literally, 'father') is used. Addressing females follows similar age-related lines:

| Address | Male | Female |
|---|---|---|
| same age | *chola* | *ajala* |
| 'grandfather' | *pola* | *mola* |
| younger | *bu* | *bumo* |
| 'father' | *pala* | *amala* |

Recently in Lhasa and other urban areas in Tibet, a new term has become the standard term of address for both males and females. This term, *genla*, literally means 'teacher' but is now used for everyone except children. It is safe to use it in all circumstances. For instance, in the example 'Hey Mister/Ms, where is the monastery?', *genla* could be used *(genla, gomba kaba du?)*. If villagers do not respond to this use of *genla*, the more traditional terms listed should be used.

## Body Language

Body language is an important aspect of any communication system. In general, being humble is highly valued in Tibetan society. Tibetans admire anyone who shows kindness, generosity, and humility in their manner. For instance if you are serving yourself at a meal, make sure you don't take the last spoonfuls of food. Make sure you leave enough for others. If you are going to sit down, try to offer the higher or the best seat to others. Sometimes when you compliment people directly or in front of

others, they may seem shy or embarrassed. This is because accepting a compliment is regarded as showing off. However, this does not mean your compliments are not appreciated.

When people meet they bow their heads slightly. When departing, heads are again bowed slightly while saying the appropriate phrases (you'll find such phrases in the Greetings section at the beginning of this chapter). The person remaining may also extend their right hand with the palm facing upwards, as if showing the way for the person departing.

When closely related people meet after a long absence, or when they part for a long time, they gently touch their foreheads together, while holding each other's hands and saying, in the case of departing, *kusu-la tujag nang rog* ('take care of your health') to which the reply is *kayrang semtel nang migaw* ('you need not worry'), or in the case of meeting *kayrang depo yimpay* ('how are you?').

When giving or receiving items, both hands are used. Alternatively the right hand is used to give or receive the item with the left hand bent towards the right elbow joint. A long white scarf called a *kata* is used in many festivals and ceremonies such as weddings, New Year and house warmings, in a similar way to flowers in Western culture. It is also used in greetings and farewells. The *kata* is given draped over both hands, and is either put around the neck of the recipient or given into their hands.

Other gestures you may see are head scratching, which shows doubt or nervousness, and shaking the index finger to show warning. Sometimes, when listening to the words of a greatly respected person, Tibetans may stick their tongue out slightly to show humbleness, respect and loyalty.

When visiting temples, visitors should take off their shoes, walk slowly and keep noise to a minimum. Hats should not be worn, nor clothing which exposes the limbs (such as singlets and shorts).

GREETINGS & CIVILITIES

# Small Talk

Most Tibetans are keen to have foreign visitors in their country, and eager to hear of happenings outside Tibet. Small gifts such as chocolates, or cigarettes help to establish new friendships.

## Meeting People
What is your name?
*kayrang gi minglâ karay ray?* ཁྱེད་རང་གི་མིང་ལ་ག་རེ་རེད།
My name is ...
*ngay minglâ ... ray* ངའི་མིང་ལ་ ----- རེད།
Pleased to meet you.
*kayrang jel-pa gawpo chung* ཁྱེད་རང་མཇལ་པ་དགའ་པོ་བྱུང་།

## Nationalities
Where are you from?
*kayrang lungbâ kanay yin?* ཁྱེད་རང་ལུང་པ་ག་ནས་ཡིན།

| I am from ... | nga ... nay yin | ང་ ----- ནས་ཡིན། |
|---|---|---|
| Africa | ahfirika | ཨཐི་རི་ག |
| Asia | asiya | ཨེ་ཤི་ཡ |
| Australia | ositaliya | ཨོསི་ཀུ་ལི་ཡ |
| Canada | kanada | ཀེན་ཌ |
| China | gyânak | རྒྱ་ནག |

| Denmark | *denmark* | དེན་མག |
| England | *injiy lungpa* | དབྱིན་ཇིའི་ལུང་པ |
| Europe | *yurop* | ཡུ་རོབ |
| Finland | *finland* | ཕིན་ལནྡ |
| France | *farenci* | ཕ་རན་སི |
| Germany | *jarman* | འཇར་མན |
| Holland | *holand* | ཧོ་ལནྡ |
| India | *gyagar* | རྒྱ་གར |
| Ireland | *ahrilen* | ཨེ་རི་ལནྡ |
| Israel | *izrael* | ཨི་ཛ་རེལ |
| Italy | *italiy* | ཨི་ཊ་ལི |
| Japan | *riybin* | རི་པིན |
| Middle East | *shar-kyil-gya-kab* | ཤར་དཀྱིལ་རྒྱལ་ཁབ |
| New Zealand | *nyu ziyland* | ཉིུ་ཟི་ལནྡ |
| Norway | *naw-way* | ནོར་ཝེ |
| Scotland | *skotland* | སོ་ཀོ་ལནྡ |
| South America | *lho amerika* | ལྷོ་ཨ་མེ་རི་ཀ |
| Spain | *spayn* | སེ་པན |
| Sweden | *swiyden* | སུ་ཝི་ཌན |
| Switzerland | *süziy* | སུད་སི |
| USA | *yu es ay/amerika* | ཡུ་ཨེས་ཨེ |
| Wales | *waylz* | ཝེ་ལས |

## Age

How old are you?
  *kayrang-lo kâtsay yin?*  ཁྱེད་རང་ལོ་ག་ཚད་ཡིན།

I am … years old.     *nga lo … yin*        ང་ལོ་ ⋯⋯ ཡིན།

  18                  *jop-gyay*           བཅོ་བརྒྱད་

  25                  *nyishu tsay-nga*    ཉི་ཤུ་རྩ་ལྔ་

(See the Numbers & Amounts chapter, page 140, for your particular age.)

## *Occupations*

What do you do (for a living)?

  *kayrang laygâ karay nâng*      ཁྱེད་རང་ལས་ཀ་ག་རེ་གནང་གི་ཡོད།
  *giy-yaw?*

I am a/an …          *nga … yin*           ང་ ⋯⋯ ཡིན།

| | | |
|---|---|---|
| actor | *tâb tönpa* | བཤད་གཞས་སྟོན་པ། |
| artist | *rimo khen* | རི་མོ་མཁན། |
| business person | *tsongpa* | ཚོང་པ། |
| doctor | *âmchi* | ཨེམ་རྗེ། |
| engineer | *sotay uchen* | བཟོ་གྲྭའི་དབུ་ཆེན། |
| factory worker | *sotay layka chay-khen* | བཟོ་གྲྭའི་ལས་ཀ་བྱེད་མཁན། |
| farmer | *shing-pâ* | ཞིང་པ། |
| journalist | *tsagbar gya-khen* | ཚགས་པར་རྒྱགས་མཁན། |
| lawyer | *thrim tsöpa* | ཁྲིམས་རྩོད་པ། |
| manual worker | *ngay-tsöl layka chay-khen* | ངལ་རྩོལ་ལས་ཀ་བྱེད་མཁན། |
| mechanic | *trulay pa* | འཕྲུལ་ལས་པ། |
| musician | *rolja tong-khen* | རོལ་ཆ་གཏོང་མཁན། |
| nurse | *nay yaw* | ནད་གཡོག |

| | | |
|---|---|---|
| office worker/clerk | drung-yig | དྲུང་ཡིག |
| scientist | tsen-rig pa | ཚན་རིག་པ |
| secretary | drung-yig | དྲུང་ཡིག |
| student | lob-trug | སློབ་ཕྲུག |
| teacher | gegen | དགེ་རྒན |
| waiter | sedim yogbo (m) | ཟས་འགྲིམས་གཡོག་པོ/ |
| | sedim yogmo (f) | ཟས་འགྲིམས་གཡོག་མོ |
| writer | tsom-dipa | རྩོམ་བྲིས་པ |

## Religion

What is your religion?

*kayrang-giy chö-lug karay ray?* ཁྱེད་རང་གི་ཆོས་ལུགས་ག་རེ་རེད

| I am ... | *nga ... yin* | ང་ ...... ཡིན |
|---|---|---|
| Buddhist | *nâng-pa* | ནང་པ |
| Catholic | *yeshu catoliy* | ཡེ་ཤུ་ཀ་ཏོ་ལི |
| Christian | *yeshu* | ཡེ་ཤུ |
| Hindu | *hindu* | ཧིན་དུ |
| Jewish | *jewish* | ཇུ་ཨི་ཤི |
| Muslim | *kâche* | ཁ་ཆེ |
| not religious | *chö khay-milen-kyen* | ཆོས་ཁས་ལེན་མི་ལེན་མཁན |

## Family

Are you married?

*kayrâng châng-sa kyön tsabay?* ཁྱེད་རང་བཟའ་ཚང་སྐྱོན་ཚར་པས

I am single.

*nga miy-hrâng yin* ང་མི་རང་ཡིན

How many children do you
have?
   *kayrâng-la pugu kâtsay yö?* ཁྱེད་རང་ལ་ཕུ་གུ་ག་ཚོད་ཡོད།

I don't have any children.
   *nga-la pugu may* ང་ལ་ཕུ་གུ་མེད།

I have a daughter/son.
   *nga-la bumo chig/bu chig yö* ང་ལ་བུ་མོ་གཅིག / བུ་གཅིག་ཡོད།

How many brothers/sisters
do you have?
   *kayrâng-la pingya bu/pingya* ཁྱེད་རང་ལ་སྤུན་ཀྱ་བུ /

   *bumo kâtsay yö?* སྤུན་ཀྱ་བུ་མོ་ག་ཚོད་ཡོད།

Is your husband/wife here?
   *kayrâng-giy kyoka/kyeman day* ཁྱེད་རང་གི་སྐྱོ་ག /

   *yo-raypay?* སྐྱེ་དམན་འདིར་ཡོད་རེད་པས།

Do you have a boyfriend/
girlfriend?
   *kayrâng-la togpo/togmo yöpay?* ཁྱེད་རང་ལ་གྲོགས་པོ/གྲོགས་མོ་ཡོད་པས།

| | | |
|---|---|---|
| aunt | *a-nay* | ཨ་ནེ |
| brother | *pingya bu* | སྤུན་རྒྱ་བུ |
| children | *pugu* | ཕུ་གུ |
| daughter | *bumo* | བུ་མོ |
| family | *nâng-miy* | ནང་མི |
| father | *papha* | པཕ |
| father-in-law | *sa-tsâng-giy papha* | བཟའ་ཚང་གི་པཕ |
| grandfather | *popo* | པོ་པོ |
| grandmother | *momo* | མོ་མོ |
| husband | *kyoka* | ཁྱོ་ག |
| mother | *ama* | ཨ་མ |
| mother-in-law | *satsâng-giy ama* | བཟའ་ཚང་གི་ཨ་མ |
| sister | *pingya bumo* | སྤུན་རྒྱ་བུ་མོ |
| son | *bu* | བུ |
| uncle | *ahshâng/aku* | ཨ་ཞང་/ཨ་ཁུ |
| wife | *kyeman* | སྐྱེ་དམན |

## Feelings

| | | |
|---|---|---|
| I ... | *nga ...* | |
|   am angry | *lung lâng giy du* | རླུང་ལངས་གི་འདུག |
|   am cold | *khya giy du* | བཁྱགས་གི་འདུག |
|   am grateful | *la kâtin chenpo yin* | ང་ལ་བཀའ་དྲིན་ཆེན་པོ་ཡིན |

| am happy | kyipo du | ད་སྐྱིད་པོ་འདུག |
| am hot | tsawa tsi giy du | ང་ཚ་བ་ཚིག་གི་འདུག |
| am hungry | throgaw-tog giy du | ང་གྲོད་ཁོག་ལྟོགས་ཀྱི་འདུག |
| am in a hurry | tewa yö | ང་འཕྲ་བ་ཡོད། |
| am right | tâgtâg ray | ང་དྲང་དྲག་རེད། |
| am sad | sem kyo-giy du | ང་སེམས་སྐྱོ་གི་འདུག |
| am sleepy | nyi ku giy du | ང་གཉིད་ཀུག་གི་འདུག |
| am sorry (condolence) | lo-phâm yö | ང་བློ་ཕམ་ཡོད། |
| am thirsty | ka kom-giy du | ང་ཁ་སྐོམ་གྱི་འདུག |
| am tired | kâlay ka giy du | ང་དགའ་ལས་ཁ་གི་འདུག |
| am well | depo yin | ང་བདེ་པོ་ཡིན། |
| am worried | semdel lâng giy du | ང་སེམས་འཁྲལ་ལངས་གི་འདུག |

## Opinions

| I ... | ngay ... | |
| agree | mothün yö | ངས་མོས་མཐུན་ཡོད། |
| don't agree | mothün may | ངས་མོས་མཐུན་མེད། |

| This/It ... | diy ... | |
| is good | yâgpo du | འདི་ལྱག་པོ་འདུག |
| isn't good | yâgpo mindu | འདི་ལྱག་པོ་མི་འདུག |

| Is this good? | diy yâgpo dugay? | འདི་ལྱག་པོ་འདུག་གས། |
| I like Tibetan food. | nga pöbay kalala gabo yö | ང་བོད་པའི་ཁ་ལག་ལ་དགའ་པོ་ཡོད། |

## *Language Difficulties*

I don't speak …
   *… shing-giy may*       ……ཤེས་ཀྱི་མེད།

I speak a little …
   *… de-tsi shing-giy yö*    ……དེ་ཙམ་ཤེས་ཀྱི་ཡོད།

Do you speak …?
   *kayrâng … shing-giy yawbay?*  ཁྱེད་རང་……ཤེས་ཀྱི་ཡོད་པས།

| I speak … | *nga … shing-giy yö* ངས་……ཤེས་ཀྱི་ཡོད།| |
|---|---|---|
| Arabic | *arab-kay* | ཨ་རབ་སྐད། |
| Chinese | *gyami-kay* | རྒྱ་མི་སྐད། |
| Danish | *denmark-kay* | དེན་མཁ་སྐད། |
| Dutch | *holand-kay* | ཧོ་ལན་ད་སྐད། |
| English | *injiy-kay* | དབྱིན་ཇི་སྐད། |
| Finnish | *finland-kay* | ཕིན་ལནྜ་སྐད། |
| French | *farensi-kay* | ཕ་རེན་སི་སྐད། |
| German | *jarman-kay* | འཇར་མན་སྐད། |
| Greek | *giyreek-kay* | གྲི་རིག་སྐད། |
| Italian | *italiy-kay* | ཨི་ཊ་ལི་སྐད། |
| Japanese | *rupin-kay* | རུ་པིན་སྐད། |
| Norwegian | *naw-way-kay* | ནོར་ཝེ་སྐད། |
| Russian | *urusu-kay* | ཨུ་རུ་སུ་སྐད། |
| Spanish | *spayn-kay* | སེ་པཱན་སྐད། |
| Swedish | *swiyden-kay* | སུད་ཌེན་སྐད། |

I understand.
   *ha ko song*        ཧ་གོ་སོང་།

I don't understand.
   *ha ko-masong*     ཧ་གོ་མ་སོང་།

SMALL TALK

Do you understand?
*ha-ko song ngay?*　　　ཧ་གོ་སོང་ངས།

Could you repeat that?
*te yâng-kyar soong rog nâng?*　དེ་ཡང་སྐྱར་གསུང་རོགས་གནང་།

Could you speak more
slowly please?
*tâtung kalay-kalay soong
nâng dâng?*　　　དདུང་ལེར་ག་ལེར་གསུང་གནང་དང་།

Please show me (in this
book).
*(tep diy-nâng) tön nâng dâng*　ང་ལ་(དེབ་འདི་དི་ནང་ལ་)སྟོན་གནང་དང་།

I will look for it in this book.
*ngay teb-diy-nâng-la
ta-giy yin*　　　ངས་དེབ་འདི་དི་ནང་ལ་བལྟ་གི་ཡིན།

How do you say …?
*… kâday lâb gaw ray?*　　　་་་ གང་འདས་ལབ་དགོས་རེད།

What does … mean?
*…-giy töntâg karay ray?*　　　་་་ གི་དོན་དག་ག་རེ་རེད།

What does this mean?
*diy tön-tâg karay ray?*　　　འདི་དི་དོན་དག་ག་རེ་རེད།

## Interests

What do you do in your spare
time?
*kayrâng thoog tepö-kâb karay
nâng-giy yö?*　　　ཁྱེད་རང་ཐུགས་སྦྱངས་དལ་པོའི་སྐབས་ག་རེ་གནང་གི་ཡོད།

I like …　　　*nga … -la kâpo yö*　　　ང་་་་ ལ་དགའ་པོ་ཡོད།

I don't like …　　　*nga … -la kâpo may*　　　ང་་་་ ལ་དགའ་པོ་མེད།

| Do you like …? | kayrâng … -la kâpo yaw bay? | ཁྱེད་རང་ ⋯⋯ ལ་དགའ་པོ་ཡོད་པ་ས། |
| discos | diskoz | ཌིས་ཀོ |
| films | log-nyan | གློག་བརྙན |
| going shopping | trom-la droyag | ཁྲོམ་ལ་འགྲོ་ཡག |
| music | rölja | རོལ་ཆ |
| playing games | tsemo | རྩེད་མོ |
| playing sport | tsemo | རྩེད་མོ |
| reading | tep lo-yag | དེབ་ཀློག་ཡག |
| travelling | châm-châm droyag | འཆམ་འཆམ་འགྲོ་ཡག |
| watching football | kâng-ball tâyag | རྐང་པོལ་བལྟ་ཡག |
| watching TV | soogtong nyan-tin tâyag/tiy-viy | གཟུགས་མཐོང་བརྙན་འཕྲིན་བལྟ་ཡག／ ཏི་ཝི |

## Some Useful Phrases

What is this called?
   *diyla karay sa?*     འདི་ལ་ག་རེ་ཟ།

Do you live here?
   *kayrâng-day shoog-giy*     ཁྱེད་རང་འདིར་བཞུགས་ཀྱི་ཡོད་པ་ས།
   *yo bay?*

Do you like it here?
   *kayrâng-day kyibo dugay?*     ཁྱེད་རང་འདིར་སྐྱིད་པོ་འདུག་གས།

Yes, a lot.
   *kyibo shayta du*     སྐྱིད་པོ་ཤིན་ཏུ་འདུག

# Getting Around

Getting around in Tibet to see the awe-inspiring scenery and temples can be achieved in a variety of ways. For longer distances buses, minibuses, taxis or hire-vehicles are available. For the energetic, bicycles or walking are also options.

## *Finding Your Way*

How do I get to…?
 *…-la ka tesi dro gawray?*   ་་་ལ་གང་འདུས་འགྲོ་དགོས་རེད།
Is it far?
 *tha-ringpo yaw raybay?*   ཐག་རིང་པོ་ཡོད་རེད་པས།
Can I walk there?
 *gompa gyâb thub-giy raybay?*  གོམ་པ་བརྒྱབ་ཐུབ་ཀྱི་རེད་པས།
Can you show me (on the map)?
 *(sabta diy-nang) tön rog nâng?*  (ས་བཀྲ་འདི་ནང་)སྟོན་རོགས་གནང་།

## *Directions*

| | | |
|---|---|---|
| east | *shar* | ཤར་ |
| west | *nub* | ནུབ་ |

| | | |
|---|---|---|
| north | *châng* | བྱང་ |
| south | *lho* | ལྷོ་ |
| straight ahead | *shâr-gya* | ཤར་རྒྱག |
| (on the) left | *yön cholâ* | གཡོན་ཕྱོགས་ལ་ |
| (on the) right | *yay cholâ* | གཡས་ཕྱོགས་ལ་ |
| at the next corner | *sur phâgay* | ཟུར་ཕ་གིར་ |
| at the next turn off | *lâm-kyog jemay tsa la* | ལམ་ཁྱོག་རྗེས་མའི་རྩ་ལ་ |
| at the traffic lights | *lâmton logshü trila* | ལམ་སྟོན་ལྡོག་བཤུད་འཁྲིའི་ཁྲིལ་ལ་ |

| | | |
|---|---|---|
| here | *day* | འདིར་ |
| there | *phâgiy* | ཕ་གིར་ |
| behind | *gyâblâ* | རྒྱབ་ལ་ |
| in front | *dünlâ* | མདུན་ལ་ |
| near | *triylâ* | འཁྲིས་ལ་ |
| far | *tha ringpo* | ཐག་རིང་པོ་ |
| opposite | *phâchog* | ཕར་ཕྱོགས་ |
| inside | *nânglâ* | ནང་ལ་ |
| outside | *chilolâ* | ཕྱི་ལོག་ལ་ |

## *Buying Tickets*

I want to buy a ticket to …
  *nga … dro-yagiy pâsay
  nyo-goyö*

ང་ ་ ་འགྲོ་ཡག་གི་པ་སེ་ཉོ་དགོས་ཡོད།

Where is the office to buy
bus tickets?
  *motay pâsay nyosay
  lay-gung kâba yawray?*

མོ་ཊའི་པ་སེ་ཉོ་སའི་ལས་ཁུངས་ག་པར་ཡོད་རེད།

| How much is the ticket to …? | … -lâ dro-yagiy pâsay gawn kâdzay ray? | འབར་འགྲོ་ཡག་གི་པ་སེར་གོང་ག་ཚོད་རེད། |
|---|---|---|
| Gyantse | gyân-dze | རྒྱལ་རྩེ། |
| Shigatse | shigâtse | གཞིས་ཀ་རྩེ། |
| Ganden | gânden | དགའ་ལྡན། |

I'd like a one-way ticket.
*pha droyâg chig-pö pâsay gaw*  ཕར་འགྲོ་ཡག་གཅིག་པོའི་པ་སེ་དགོས།
I'd like a return ticket.
*phâdro tsulog nyikay pâsay gaw*  ཕར་འགྲོ་ཚུར་ལོག་གཉིས་ཀའི་པ་སེ་དགོས།
Can I reserve a place?
*dösa ngon-nay nyo chogiy rebay?*  སྟོད་ས་སྔོན་ནས་ཉོ་ཆོག་གི་རེད་པས།
Is it completely full?
*cha-tsâng khâng tsa rebay?*  ཆ་ཚང་ཁང་ཚར་རེད་པས།
Please refund my ticket.
*pâsay-ngu tsur logrog nâng*  པ་སེའི་དངུལ་ཚུར་ལོག་རོགས་གནང་།

## Air
When is the next flight to …?
*… dro yagi nâmdru jema-de kâdu ray?*  འགྲོ་ཡག་གི་གནམ་གྲུ་རྗེས་མ་དེ་ག་དུས་རེད།

How long does the flight take?
    *nâmdru-nâng gyün ringlo drogaw ray?*    གནམ་གྲུ་ནང་རྒྱུན་རིང་ལོས་འགྲོ་དགོས་རེད།

| aeroplane/plane | *nâmdru* | གནམ་གྲུ |
| airport | *nâmtâng* | གནམ་ཐང་ |
| airport tax | *nâmtâng tel* | གནམ་ཐང་ཁྲལ |
| boarding pass | *dösay pâsay* | སྡོད་ས་པ་སེ |
| customs | *kâgo laygung/gotel laygung* | བཀག་སྒོ་ལས་ཁུངས/སྒོ་ཁྲལ་ལས་ཁུངས |

## Bicycle

In Lhasa, the best means of transport is a bicycle. These can usually be hired from the smaller hotels.

Do you hire bicycles?
    *gâng-gâriy laya yöbay?*    ཀང་སྒོ་རི་ལ་གླ་ལ་ཡོད་པ་ས།

| How much is it per ...? | ... *rayrayla lâja kâtsö ray?* | ... རེ་རེ་ལ་གླ་ཆ་ག་ཚོད་རེད། |
| hour | *chutsö* | ཆུ་ཚོད |
| day | *nyimâ* | ཉིནམ |
| week | *sa-khor/düntâg* | བཟའ་སྐོར/བདུན་ཕྲག |
| month | *dawa* | ཟླ་བ |

| It costs ... yuan per day. | *nyimâ rayray gawmo ... ray* | ཉིན་མ་རེ་རེ་ ... སྒོར་མོ་རེད། |
| five | *nga* | ལྔ |
| ten | *chu* | བཅུ |

Do you have a bicycle for
hire now?
    *tânda gâng-gâriy chig lâya*    ད་ལྟ་ཤར་སྐྱ་རི་ལ་གླ་ལག་ཡོད་པས།
    *yöbay?*

You have to leave your
passport here (as security).
    *kayrang-ki lâg-teb day*    ཁྱེད་རང་གི་ལག་དེབ་འདིར་བཞག་དགོས་རེད།
    *shâgoray*

Does this road lead to …?
    *… droyagiy lâmga di rebay?*    ····· འགྲོ་ཡག་གི་ལམ་ག་འདི་རེད་པས།

Can you fix this bicycle?
    *gâng-gâriy-diy so thup-kiy*    ཤར་སྐྱ་རི་འདི་བཟོ་ཐུབ་ཀྱི་རེད་པས།
    *rebay?*

It's got a puncture.
    *khorlo dhö sha*    འཁོར་ལོ་བཏོལ་ཤག

| | | |
|---|---|---|
| brakes | *kha kâyag* | ཁ་བཀག་ལག |
| chain | *khorlö châgtâg* | འཁོར་ལོའི་ལྕགས་ཐག |
| tools | *lâgcha* | ལག་ཆ |
| tyre | *gyigiy khorlo* | འགྱིག་གི་འཁོར་ལོ |
| tube | *khorlo nângiy-shub* | འཁོར་ལོ་ནང་གི་ཤུབས |

## Hiring Vehicles

Vehicle rental is becoming the most popular way of getting
around in Tibet, especially for those travellers with limited time.
There are numerous agencies dealing with the rental of
landcruisers, jeeps and minibuses in Lhasa, and a few are also
based in Shigatse. It's a good idea to reach an agreement that
payment is delivered in two instalments, one before setting off
and one on successful completion of the trip.

| I'd like to hire a ... | nga ... yar dhö-yö | ང་ ... གཡར་འདོད་ཡོད། |
|---|---|---|
| jeep | jip | ཇིབ། |
| landcruiser | mota/land krusâ | མོ་ཊ། ལེནྚ་ཀུ་ར་སུ། |
| minibus | dru-kyel mota chung chung | འགྲུལ་སྐྱེལ་མོ་ཊ་ཆུང་ཆུང་། |

How much does it cost per kilometre?
 kilometa ray-rayla gong ga-tsay nay-kiy ray?

གི་ལོ་མི་ཊར་རེ་རེ་ལ་གོང་ག་ཚད་གནད་ཀྱི་རེད།

I'll pay half now, and half at the end of the trip.
 la chekâ dânta tay-kiy yin, chekâ jayma dro-tshar-nay tay-kiy yin

ལ་ཕྱེད་ཀ་ད་ལྟ་སྤྲྱད་ཀྱི་ཡིན།
ཕྱེད་ཀ་རྗེས་མ་འགྲོ་ཚར་ནས་སྤྲྱད་ཀྱི་ཡིན།

I'd like to see the car.
 nga mota mig ta-dhö yö

ང་མོ་ཊ་མིག་བལྟ་འདོད་ཡོད།

I'd like to meet the driver.
 nga mota tong-khen thoog-dhö yö

ང་མོ་ཊ་གཏོང་མཁན་ཐུག་འདོད་ཡོད།

How many people does the vehicle take?
 motay-nâng mi ga-tsay shong-giy ray?

མོ་ཊའི་ནང་མི་ག་ཚད་ཤོང་གི་རེད།

## Bus & Minibus

Bus travel in Tibet is slow and gruelling. Most bus services originate in Lhasa and connect the capital with Shigatse, Tsetang and the border. Many privately run minibuses service areas not visited by public buses. Minibuses are cheaper than public buses as foreigners are only charged local prices.

Where is the bus (stop) for ...?
   ...-lâ dro-ngen giy mota kâba    ལ་འགྲོ་མཁན་གྱི་མོ་ཊ་ག་པར་ཡོད་རེད།
   yawray?

| What time is the ... bus? | mota ... chutsö kâtsay- la drogiy ray? | མོ་ཊ་ ⸺ ཆུ་ཚོད་ག་ཚོད་ལ་རེད། |
|---|---|---|
| next | jema-te | རྗེས་མ་དེ |
| first | tângpo | དང་པོ |
| last | thama-te | མཐའ་མ་དེ |

Where is this (bus) going?
   (mota diy) kâba drugiy ray?   མོ་ཊ་འདི་ག་པར་འགྲོ་གི་རེད།
Will it go to ...?
   ...-lâ drugiy rebay?    ⸺ ལ་འགྲོ་གི་རེད་པས།

What time will the bus to ... arrive?
   ... droyakiy mota chudzö    འགྲོ་ཡག་གི་མོ་ཊ་ཆུ་ཚོད་ག་ཚོད་ལ་འབྱོར་གྱི་རེད།
   kâdzay jorgiy ray?

What time will it leave ...?
   ... chutsö kâtsay    ཆུ་ཚོད་ག་ཚོད་ལ་འགྲོ་གི་རེད།
   drugiy ray?
    tomorrow    sânyi    སང་ཉིན

| today | *thâriy* | དེ་རིང་ |
| this evening (late afternoon) | *thogong* | དོ་གོང་ |

Could you let me know when
we get to …?
    *… -la lebdü nga-la len kyelrog nâng?* ང་ཚོ་ ... ལ་སྲེབས་དུས་ང་ལ་ལེན་སྐྱེལ་རོགས་གནང་།

I want to get off!
    *nga mar bâb-kiy yin!* ང་མར་བབས་ཀྱི་ཡིན།

## Taxi

Taxis are readily available for travel outside Lhasa, but are
generally not used for travel within the city.

Where can I find a taxi?
    *dâla tong-yakiy modra kâba yawray?* དཔལ་འབྱོར་གཏོང་ཡ་ཀྱི་མོ་ཊ་ག་པར་ཡོད་རེད།

Please hire us a taxi.
    *mota-chig dâla tong nâng-dâng* མོ་ཊ་གཅིག་དཔལ་འབྱོར་གཏོང་གནང་དང་།

Can you take me to …?
    *… -la kyelrog nâng?* ... ལ་སྐྱེལ་རོགས་གནང་།

I want a taxi to the airport.
    *nâmthâng-bar mota chig gawgiy du* གནམ་ཐང་བར་མོ་ཊ་གཅིག་དགོས་ཀྱི་འདུག

We want to go to Nepal.
    *ngândzo phay-yülâ droken-yin* ང་ཚོ་བལ་ཡུལ་ལ་འགྲོ་མཁན་ཡིན།

GETTING AROUND

How much will it cost?
*lâja kâtsay nay-giy ray?*　 སླ་ཆ་ག་ཚོད་གནད་ཀྱི་རེད།

## Instructions

Please go slowly.
*kâliy kâliy drorog nâng*　ག་ལེར་ག་ལེར་འགྲོ་རོགས་ཨ།
Please go faster.
*gyopo drorog ah*　མགྱོགས་པོ་འགྲོ་ཨ།
Here is fine, thank you.
*dhay digsong, thujeche*　འདིར་འགྲིག་སོང་། ཐུགས་རྗེ་ཆེ།
The next corner, please.
*soor phâkay kâgrog nâng*　ཟུར་ཕ་གིར་བཀག་རོགས་གནད།
Continue!
*mu thü-nâng!*　མུ་མཐུད་གནད།
Please wait here.
*dhay gurog nâng*　འདིར་འགུག་རོགས་གནད།

## Some Useful Words & Phrases

| The (bus) is ... | *mota ... shâg* | མོ་ཊ་ ...... ཤག |
|---|---|---|
| delayed | *jelü teb* | རྗེས་ལུས་ཐེབས |
| cancelled | *chiten gyâb* | ཕྱིར་འཐེན་བརྒྱབ |
| on time | *dütog-ray* | དུས་ཐོག་རེད |

How long does the trip take?
*gyun ringlö dro-ya yö ray?*　རྒྱུན་རིང་ལོས་འགྲོ་ཡག་ཡོད་རེད།
Is it a direct route?
*sha-kyâg droya rebay?*　ཤར་ཀྱག་འགྲོ་ཡག་རེད་པས།
How far to go?
*tha kâtsay drugyu yawray?*　དག་ཚོད་འགྲོ་རྒྱུ་ཡོད་རེད།

**Is that seat taken?**
*kup-kyâg phâgay mi-dö-kyen* རྐུབ་ཀྱག་ཕགིར་མི་སྡོད་མཁན་ཡོད་རེད་པས།
*yaw rebay?*

**Please stop (the truck).**
*(mota) kârog nâng* མོ་ཊ་བཀག་རོགས་གནང་།

**I want to take a picture.**
*nga par chig gyâm döyö* ང་པར་གཅིག་བརྒྱབ་འདོད་ཡོད།

| | | |
|---|---|---|
| cancel | *chiten* | ཕྱིར་འཐེན་ |
| fastest route | *lâmchog gyog-shö* | ལམ་ཕྱོགས་མགྱོགས་ཤོས་ |
| 1st class | *dösa âng-rim dâng-po* | སྡོད་ས་ཨང་རིམ་དང་པོ་ |
| 2nd class | *dösa âng-rim nyipa* | སྡོད་ས་ཨང་རིམ་གཉིས་པ་ |
| horse & cart | *thega/therga* | ཐེར་ག་ |
| horse | *ta* | རྟ་ |
| jeep | *jip* | ཇིབ་ |
| man-drawn cart | *mi-dray khawlo* | མིས་གྲུད་འཁོར་ལོ་ |
| map | *sâpta* | ས་བཀྲ་ |
| minibus | *membow/dru-kye* | མེན་བོ་/ |
| | *mota chung-chung* | འགྲུལ་སྐྱེལ་མོ་ཊ་ཆུང་ཆུང་ |
| | *chung chung* | |
| nonsmoking | *thama then michog* | ཐ་མག་འཐེན་མི་ཆོག་ |
| one-way (ticket) | *pha droya chigpö* | ཕར་འགྲོ་ཡ་གཅིག་པོའི་ (པ་སེ་) |
| | *(pâsay)* | |
| return (ticket) | *phâdro tsulog nyigay* | ཕར་འགྲོ་ཚུར་ལོག་གཉིས་ཀའི་ (པ་སེ་) |
| | *(pâsay)* | |
| seat | *dösa* | སྡོད་ས་ |
| short route | *lâmchog tha-nyewa* | ལམ་ཕྱོགས་ཐག་ཉེ་བ་ |

GETTING AROUND

| | | |
|---|---|---|
| smoking | *thamâg* | བ་མག |
| ticket | *pâsay* | པ་སེ |
| timetable | *dütso raymig* | དུས་ཚོད་རེའུ་མིག |
| taxi | *taksi/dala tong-ya kiy mota* | ཊེ་སི/ད་པ་ལ་གཏོང་ཡས་མོ་ཊ |
| tractor | *tolachi/shingmö tru-khor* | ཌོ་ལ་ཇི/ཞིང་ མོ་ལ་འཁྲུལ་འཁོར |

# Accommodation

There is now a variety of accommodation available in both Lhasa and Shigatse, Tibet's second largest city, ranging from luxury to small hotels/inns.

In Tibet's small inns you can either rent a bed in a dormitory or in a private room (with two or three beds). Normally there are hotel staff assigned to each floor and you approach them first if you need anything. It is best to address all such people as *genla*. In the country, there are no hotels and you will have to either bring along your own tent or convince a villager to let you stay the night with them. Every district (*dzong* or *shen*), however, has rooms which are rented out to truck drivers and officials and sometimes travellers.

| Where is ...? | ... *kâba du?* | ག་པར་འདུག |
| a guesthouse/inn | *drön-khâng* | མགྲོན་ཁང |
| a hotel | *dru-khâng/fandian* | འགྲུལ་ཁང |

Could you write the
address down?
   *kâjâng day tirog nâng?*  ཁ་བྱང་འདིར་འབྲི་རོགས་གནང |

59

## At the Hotel
### Checking In

| | | |
|---|---|---|
| I'm going to stay for ... | nga ... day-giy yin | ང་ · · · བསྡད་ཀྱི་ཡིན། |
| one day | nyin-chig | ཉིན་གཅིག |
| two days | nyin-nyi | ཉིན་གཉིས། |
| one week | sâgor chig/düntâg chig | གཟའ་འཁོར་གཅིག/ བདུན་ཕྲག་གཅིག |

I'm not sure how long I'm staying.

nga yu-ringlö daygaw tenten may

ང་ཡུན་རིང་ལོས་བསྡད་དགོས་གཏན་གཏན་མེད།

Are there any private rooms here?

day nye-khâng kâp-tsâng dugay?

འདིར་ཉལ་ཁང་ཁབ་གཙང་འདུག་གས།

| I need ... bed(s) | nga-la nyethri ... gaw | ང་ལ་ཉལ་ཁྲི་ · · · དགོས། |
|---|---|---|
| one | chig | གཅིག |
| two | nyi | གཉིས། |
| three | sum | གསུམ |

| How much for the room/bed ...? | ... rayray-la khâng-mi/ nyethri laja kâtsay ray? | · · · རེ་རེ་ལ་ཁང་མི/ ཉལ་ཁྲི་ལག་ཆ་ཀ་ཚད་རེད། |
|---|---|---|
| per day | nyimâ | ཉིནམ |
| per week | sa-khor/dün-tâg | གཟའ་འཁོར/བདུན་ཕྲག |
| per month | dawa | ཟླབ |

| Is/Are there …? | … *dugay?* | ་འདུག་གས། |
| hot water (for washing body) | *(sugpo truya) chu tshabo* | (གཟུགས་པོ་ཁྲུས་ལས་) ཆུ་ཚ་པོ་ |
| bed bugs | *dri-shig* | འདི་ཤིག |
| a toilet | *sânchö* | གསང་སྤྱོད་ |
| a private toilet | *sânchö râng-dâg* | གསང་སྤྱོད་རང་བདག |
| a bath house | *tru-khâng* | ཁྲུས་ཁང་ |
| a restaurant | *sa-khâng* | ཟ་ཁང་ |

Can I see the room?
*nye-khâng mig-tana digiy rebay?*  ཉལ་ཁང་མིག་བལྟ་ན་འགྲིག་གི་རེད་པས།

It's fine, I'll take it.
*yâg-po du, khâng-pa-di la-giy yin*  ལེགས་པོ་འདུག། ཁང་པ་འདི་ང་ལྒུ་གི་ཡིན།

Do you have another (room)?
*nye-khâng shenda yawbay?*  ཉལ་ཁང་གཞན་དག་ཡོད་པས།

Do you have a room with a private toilet?
*sânchö rângda-kiy nyekhâng yawbay?*  གསང་སྤྱོད་རང་བདག་གི་ཉལ་ཁང་ཡོད་པས།

Do you have a room with a window?
*giy-gung yawbay nyekhang yawbay?*  སྐེ་ཁུང་ཡོད་པའི་ཉལ་ཁང་ཡོད་པས།

NB. In this last phrase, the accent on the first *yawbay* is on the first syllable *yaw*, whereas that of the second *yawbay* is on the second syllable *bay*.

| | | |
|---|---|---|
| Can I get … here? | *day … râgiy rebay?* | འདིར་…རག་གི་རེད་པས། |
| food/meals | *kala* | ཁ་ལག |
| boiled water | *chu kömâ* | ཆུ་འཁོལ་མ |



## Hotel Service

Who is it?
*su ray?* སུ་རེད།

Just a minute.
*te tsi gu-ah* ཏོག་ཙམ་སྒུགས་ཨ།

Come in.
*ya phay* ཡར་ཕེབས།

| | | |
|---|---|---|
| Where is the …? | *… kâba du?* | …ག་པར་འདུག |
| key (to my room) | *(ngay nyekhâng-kiy) dimiy* | (ངའི་ཉལ་ཁང་གི་)ལྡེ་མིག |
| dining room/ restaurant | *kala sasah/ sa-khâng* | ཁ་ལག་ཟ་ས་/ཟ་ཁང་ |
| barbershop | *tra-shâkang* | སྐྲ་བཞར་ཁང་ |
| post office | *drâg-khâng/ yig-sâmju* | སྦྲག་ཁང་/ཡིག་ཟམ་ཚུས་ |

## Requests

| | | |
|---|---|---|
| Please wake me up at … tomorrow. | *sa-nyin … nyi sayrog nâng* | སང་ཉིན་…གཉིད་སད་རོགས་གནང་། |
| five o'clock | *chutsö nga par* | ཆུ་ཚོད་ལྔ་པར་ |
| six o'clock | *chutsö dug-par* | ཆུ་ཚོད་དྲུག་པར་ |

Could you store this/these for me?
*diy/dintso nyârog nâng-gay?* འདི་/འདི་ཚོ་ཉར་རོགས་གནང་གས།

| Please give me a ... | nga la ... chig tayrog nâng | ང་ལ་་་གཅིག་སྟེར་རོགས་གནང་། |
| --- | --- | --- |
| blanket | nyay jay | ཉལ་ཆས། |
| (extra) quilt | phogay (töbâ) | ཕོགིནས་ (སྟོབ་པ) |
| sheet | châg-ta/tendzi | ཆག་དར/གྲེན་རྩེ |
| pillow | nyen-go | སྔས་མགོ |
| pillowcase | nyen-shub | སྔས་ཤུབ |

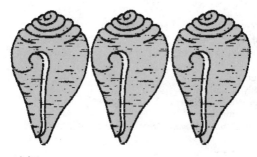

## Complaints

This room is dirty.
*nye-khâng-diy tsogpa raysha*  ཉལ་ཁང་འདི་བཙོག་པ་རེད་ཤག

| This room is too ... | nyekhâng-diy ... thra-sha | ཉལ་ཁང་འདི་་་དྲགས་ཤག |
| --- | --- | --- |
| big | chay | ཆེ |
| small | chung | ཆུང |
| noisy | kejö-tsha/amjo tsha | སྐད་ཅོར་ཚ/ཨམ་ཇོག་ཚ |

| The … doesn't work. | … diy kyön shorsha | འདི་སྐྱོན་ཤོར་སོ་ཤག |
|---|---|---|
| lamp | shuma | བུ་ཤ་མར་ |
| light bulb | shedo | ཤེལ་རྡོག |
| heater | tsalog/thrö tong-yagiy lung-gaw | ཚ་སློག/དྲོད་གཏོང་ཡག་གི་ རླུང་འགོར་ |
| TV | tensh/sugthong ngenthrin | གཟུགས་མཐོང་མཆན་རྟེན་འཕྲིན/ དེན་རི |
| telephone | kâbar | ཁ་པར་ |

| Please fix … | … soro nâng | … བཟོ་རོག་གནང་། |
|---|---|---|
| this | diy | འདི་ |
| this/the bed | nyethri diy | ཉལ་ཁྲི་འདི་ |

## Laundry

Can you wash this?
*diy tru-thub-giy rebay?*  འདི་བཀྲུ་ཐུབ་ཀྱི་རེད་པས།

Please iron these.
*dindzo uti kyön nâng-dâng*  འདི་ཚོ་ཡུར་ཏི་བརྒྱབ་གནང་དང་།

## Checking Out

| I'd like to check out … | … nga thön-giy yin | ང་ … འཐོན་གྱི་ཡིན། |
|---|---|---|
| now | dânda | ད་ལྟ་ |
| at noon | nyin-gung | ཉིན་གུང་ |
| tomorrow | sânyin | སང་ཉིན་ |

Please calculate the bill.
*ngü tsiy gyöndâ*  དངུལ་རྩིས་བརྒྱབ་དང་།

Can I leave my luggage here?
*ngay chalâg day shâna
dig-giy rebay?* ང་འི་ཅ་ལག་འདིར་བཞག་ན་འགྲིག་གི་རེད་པས།

## Some Useful Words & Phrases

May I use the kitchen?
*tâhp-tsâng baychö chay-na
dig-giy rebay?* ཐབ་ཚང་བེད་སྤྱོད་བྱེད་ན་འགྲིག་གི་རེད་པས།

Could I use the telephone?
*kâba baychö chay-na
dig-giy rebay?* ཁ་པར་བེད་སྤྱོད་བྱེད་ན་འགྲིག་གི་རེད་པས།

| | | |
|---|---|---|
| bathroom | *tru-khâng* | ཁྲུས་ཁང་ |
| bed | *nyethri* | ཉལ་ཁྲི་ |
| bed bugs | *dri-shig* | འདྲི་ཤིག |
| bill | *ngü tsiy* | དངུལ་འཛིན་ |
| blanket | *nye-jay* | ཉལ་ཆས་ |
| bug killer | *bumen* | འབུ་སྨན་ |
| candle | *yâng-la* | ཡང་ལར་ |
| clean | *tsâng-ma* | གཙང་མ་ |
| cold | *drâng-mo* | གྲང་མོ་ |
| dark | *na-gung* | ནག་ཏུང་ |
| dirty | *tsogpa* | བཙོག་པ་ |
| door | *go* | སྒོ་ |
| double bed | *mi-nyi shong-say nyethri* | མི་གཉིས་ཤོང་སའི་ཉལ་ཁྲི་ |
| fan | *lun-gaw* | རླུང་འཁོར་ |
| key | *di-miy* | ལྡེ་མིག |
| lamp | *shuma* | བཞུ་མར་ |

ACCOMMODATION

| | | |
|---|---|---|
| light bulb | shedo | ཤེལ་ཌོག |
| lock (n) | gochâg | སྒོ་ལྕགས |
| matches | musi/tsâg-ta | སུ་ཟེ/ཚག་ཏ |
| mattress | böten | འབོལ་གདན |
| pillow | nyen-go | སྔས་མགོ |
| quiet | kâgu simpo | ཁ་ཁུག་སིམ་པོ |
| radio | hruyinji/lung-drin | རུང་འཕྲིན/རླུང་འཛིན |
| (private) room | nye-khâng (kapdzang) | ཉལ་ཁང(ཁབ་གཙང) |
| sheet | châg-ta/tendzi | ཚག་དར/སྟན་རྫི |
| shower | sugpo thruya-chu/ thorchu | གཟུགས་པོ་འཁྲུ་ཡས་ཆུ/འཐོར་ཆུ |
| soap | yi-tse | ཡི་ཙེ |
| suitcase | doh-dray/gâm | རྡོག་འབྲས/སྒམ |
| table | chog-tse | ཅོག་ཙེ |
| thermos flask | chadâm | ཇ་དམ |
| TV | sugthong nyen- thrin/tensh | གཟུགས་མཐོང་བརྙན་འཕྲིན/ཏེན་ཤི |
| toilet paper | tshâng-dray shugu/sânchö shugu | གཙང་སྒྲའི་ཤོག་གུ/གསང་སྤྱོད་ཤོག་གུ |
| towel | ajo/trü-ray | ཨ་ཇོ/ཕྲུས་རས |
| wash basin | tongben | དོང་བེན/ཁྲུས་གཞོང |
| water – hot/cold | chu drângmo/tshâbo | ཆུ་གྲང་མོ/ཆུ་ཚ་བོ |
| window | gaykung | སྐེ་ཁུང |

# Around Town

Lhasa is the heart and soul of Tibet, probably because it is the home of the Dalai Lamas, and the destination of devout pilgrimages. The *Potala* is a vast white and ochre fortress which dominates Lhasa, and deserves a place as one of the wonders of Eastern architecture. The most sacred and active of the Buddhist temples in Lhasa is the Jokhang. The route surrounding this temple (circumambulation route), the *Barkhor*, is the holiest of its kind in Lhasa.

Modern Lhasa is divided clearly into a western Chinese area, and an eastern Tibetan area. For those who have already visited China, the Tibetan sector is the best area to be based in.

| I'm looking for the/a … | … kâba yawmay tagiy yaw | ག་བར་ཡོད་མེད་བཙལ་གི་ཡོད། |
|---|---|---|
| art gallery | lagtsel demtön-khâng | ལག་རྩལ་བགྲེམས་སྟོན་ཁང་ |
| bank | ngü-khâng | དངུལ་ཁང་ |
| church | lha-khâng | ལྷ་ཁང་ |
| city centre | drong-kay-kil | གྲོང་ཁྱེར་དཀྱིལ་ |
| … embassy | … shung-tsâb-khâng | གཞུང་ཚབ་ཁང་ |

67

| | | |
|---|---|---|
| hotel | *dru-khâng* | བགྲུལ་ཁང་ |
| market | *trom* | བཙོང་ |
| museum | *demtön-khâng* | བགྲེམས་སྟོན་ཁང་ |
| police | *korsung-wa* | སྐོར་སྲུང་བ |
| post office | *dra-khâng* | སྦྲག་ཁང་ |
| public toilet | *mi-mâng sânchö* | མི་དམངས་གསང་སྤྱོད་ |
| restaurant | *sa-khâng* | ཟ་ཁང་ |
| telephone centre | *kâba lay-khung* | ཁ་པར་ལས་ཁུངས |
| tourist informa- tion office | *yukor tocham-giy laykhung* | ཡུལ་སྐོར་སྟོ་འཆམས་གྱི་ལས་ཁུངས |

(See Getting Around, page 48, for directions.)

(See Getting Around, page 48, for directions.)

## At the Bank

I want to exchange some
money.
   *nga ngü jaygaw yö*  ང་དངུལ་བརྗེ་དགོས་ཡོད།
I want to change travellers'
cheques.
   *nga drushü ngü -dzin jaygaw yö*  ང་བགྲུལ་བཞུད་དངུལ་འཛིན་བརྗེ་དགོས་ཡོད།

Please change this money to
yuan.
   *ngü diy yuan lâ jay-ronâng*  དངུལ་འདི་ལུ་ཡུཨན་ལ་བརྗེ་རོགས་གནང་།
Please change this travellers'
cheque.
   *drüshu ngü dzin diy
   jay-ronâng*  བགྲུལ་བཞུད་དངུལ་འཛིན་འདི་བརྗེ་རོགས་གནང་།

What is the exchange rate?
   *ngü jaypo gyab-pay gong
   kâtsay ray?*      དངུལ་བརྗེ་པོ་བརྒྱབ་པའི་གོང་ཚོད་ག་ཚད་རེད།

How many yuan per
dollar?
   *dollar rayla yuan kâtsay ray?*      ཌོ་ལར་རེ་ལ་ཡུ་ཨན་ག་ཚོད་རེད།

Can I have money transferred
here from my bank?
   *ngay ngü chö-say ngu khâng-
   nay ngü day tong thupkiy
   raybay?*      ངའི་དངུལ་འཚོལ་སའི་དངུལ་ཁང་ནས་དངུལ་
འདིར་གཏང་ཐུབ་ཀྱི་རེད་པས།

How long will it take to
arrive here/there ?
   *day/phâgay lebpa-la gyün
   ringlö gâkiray?*      འདིར།/ཕ་གེར་སླེབས་པ་ལ་རྒྱུན་རིང་ལོས་
འགའ་གི་རེད།

I'm expecting some money
from …
   *nga la … nay ngü leb-kiy yö*      ང་ལ་ ⋯ ནས་དངུལ་སླེབས་ཀྱི་ཡོད།

Has my money arrived yet?
   *than-da ngay ngü leb
   song-ngay?*      ད་ལྟ་ངའི་དངུལ་སླེབས་སོང་ངས།

## Some Useful Words

| | | |
|---|---|---|
| bank | *ngü-khâng* | དངུལ་ཁང་ |
| black market | *nâg-tsong* | ནག་ཚོང་ |
| cashier | *ngü-nye* | དངུལ་གཉེར་ |
| credit card | *ngü tsâb lâgkhay* | དངུལ་ཚབ་ལག་ཁྱེར་ |
| currency exchange | *ngöjay gyâb* | དངུལ་བརྗེ་བརྒྱབ་ |
| exchange | *jaypo gyâb* | བརྗེ་པོ་བརྒྱབ་ |

AROUND TOWN

| money | ngü | ངུལ |
| signature | sa-yig | ས་ཡིག |
| travellers' cheques | drushü ngü -dzin | འགྲུལ་བཞུད་ངུལ་འཛིན |

## At the Post Office

| I would like to send a ... | nga ...-chig tâng-gaw yaw | ... གཅིག་གཏང་དགོས་ཡོད |
| letter | yige | ཡིག་གེ |
| parcel | chalâg | ཅ་ལག |
| postcard | dâshog | ཕྲག་ཤོག |
| telegram | tar | ཏར |

I'd like some stamps.
nga-la tikasi (dâg-tâg) ka-shay-shig gaw      ང་ལ་ཊི་ཀ་སི་ (ཕྲག་རྟགས ) ཁ་ཤས་ཤིག་དགོས
     ཀྱི་འདུག

How much is the postage?
dag-la kâtsay ray?      ཕྲག་ལ་ག་ཚོད་རེད

## Some Useful Words

| aerogram | nâmthog tonyâg dâg-sho/nâmdag yigsho | གནམ་ཐོག་གཏོང་ཡག་ལས་ཕྲག་ཤོག / གནམ་ཕྲག་ལ་ཡིག་ཤོག |
| air mail | nâmthog ton-yagi dâg/nâmdag | གནམ་ཐོག་གཏོང་ལས་ཕྲག / གནམ་ཕྲག |
| envelope | yikog | ཡིག་ཀོག |
| mailbox | dâ-gâm | ཕྲག་སྒམ |
| parcel | chalâg | ཅ་ལག |
| registered mail | teb-kyel dâg | དེབ་སྐྱེལ་ཕྲག |
| stamp | tikasi/dâg-tâg | ཊི་ཀ་སི / ཕྲག་རྟགས |
| surface mail | sathog ton-yâgi dâg | ས་ཐོག་གཏོང་ལས་ཡ་གི་ཕྲག |

AROUND TOWN

## Telephone

I want to call …
    *nga … -la kapa tân-gaw yaw*     ང་···ལ་ཁ་པར་གཏང་དགོས་ཀྱི་ཡོད།

I want to speak for three
minutes.
    *karma-sum kecha shegö yaw*     སྐར་མ་གསུམ་སྐད་ཆ་བཤད་དགོས་ཡོད།

How much does a three-
minute call cost?
    *karma-sum kecha shena gong*     སྐར་མ་གསུམ་སྐད་ཆ་བཤད་ན་གོང་གཙོང་རེད།
    *kâtsay ray?*

How much does each extra
minute cost?
    *karma thöpa rayray-la gong*     སྐར་མ་ལྷག་པ་རེ་རེ་ལ་གོང་ག་ཚོད་རེད།
    *kâtsay ray?*

**AROUND TOWN**

I want to make a reverse-
charges phone call.
    *gong phâchog-nay tay göyak-giy*     གོང་ཕ་ཕྱོགས་ནས་སྤྲད་དགོས་ལ་གི་ཁ་པར་
    *kapa chig tong gö-yaw*     ཞིག་གཏང་དགོས་ཡོད།
I'd like to speak to …
    *nga …-la kecha she-gaw yaw*     ང་···ལ་སྐད་ཆ་བཤད་དགོད་ཡོད།

Hello, do you speak English?
    *tashidelek, kayrang injiy kay*     བཀྲ་ཤིས་བདེ་ལེགས། ཁྱེད་རང་དབྱིན་ཇི་སྐད་
    *shingiy yawpay?*     ཤེས་ཀྱི་ཡོད་པས།
Hello, is … there?
    *tashi delek, …-la shoog dugay?*     བཀྲ་ཤིས་བདེ་ལེགས། ···བཞུགས་འདུག་གས།
Yes, he/she is here.
    *la, khong shoog du*     ལགས། ཁོང་བཞུགས་འདུག

One moment, please.
  *te-tsi gu nâng-rog*  ཏོག་ཙམ་བསྒུག་གནང་རོགས།

It's engaged.
  *kâbar dewa raysha*  ཁ་པར་བྲེལ་བ་རེད་འདུག

Operator, I've been cut off.
  *khapa laychay-pa, nga kecha*  ཁ་པར་ལས་བྱེད་པ། ང་སྐད་ཆ་བཤད་ཀྱི་འདུག་གི་ཁ་པར་ཆ་ཚམས་ཆད་སོང་།
  *shay-ki shay-ki kapa tsham*
  *chesong*

## Some Useful Words

| engaged (busy) | *dewa* | བྲེལ་བ |
| operator | *kâpar laychay-pa* | ཁ་པར་ལས་བྱེད |
| person to person | *mi-dâng mi tug-nay* | མི་དང་མི་ཐུག་ནས |
| public telephone | *chipay kâpa* | སྤྱི་པའི་ཁ་པར |
| reverse charges | *gong pha-chog nay tröyak* | གོང་ཕ་ཕྱོགས་ནས་སྤྲོད་ཡག |
| telephone | *kâpa* | ཁ་པར |
| telephone booth | *kâpa tong-say khâng-chung* | ཁ་པར་གཏོང་སའི་ཁང་ཆུང |
| telephone card | *kapa tong-yakiy la-khay* | ཁ་པར་གཏོང་ཡག་གི་ལག་ཁྱེར |

## Sightseeing

Is there a tourist office?
*yükor trochâm-giy lay-khun yaw raybay?*  ཡུལ་སྐོར་སློ་འཆམ་གྱི་ལས་ཁུངས་ཡོད་རེད་པས།

What's that ...?   ... *phâgiy karay ray?*  ...... ཕ་གི་ག་རེ་རེད།
building   *khâng-pa*  ཁང་པ
monument   *drensö-ten*  དྲན་གསོའི་རྟེན
place   *sacha*  ས་ཆ

How old is it?
*nying-lö ray?*  དེ་སྙིང་ལོས་རེད།

What time does it open/close?
*chutsö kâtsö-la go che/gyâb giy ray?*  ཆུ་ཚོད་ག་ཚོད་ལ་སྒོ་ཕྱེ་/སྒོ་བརྒྱབ་གི་རེད།

Where can I get a local map?
*sânay-kiy sâta kânay ragiy ray?*  ས་གནས་ཀྱི་ས་བཀྲག་ནས་རག་གི་རེད།

Is it OK if I take a photo?
*par gyâbna digiy-rebay?*  པར་རྒྱབ་ན་འགྲིགས་གི་རེད་པས།

Can I take your photograph?
*kayrâng par gyâb-na digiy rebay?*  ཁྱེད་རང་པར་བརྒྱབ་ན་འགྲིགས་གི་རེད་པས།

Could you take a photograph of me?
*kayrâng-kiy nga par-chig gyâb nângda?*  ཁྱེད་རང་གིས་ང་པར་ཅིག་བརྒྱབ་གནང་དང་།

Would you like a copy?
*kayrâng par gawpay?*  ཁྱེད་རང་པར་དགོས་པས།

I'll send you one.
    *ngay chig tâng yong gaw*    ངས་གཅིག་གཏང་ཡོང་གོ
What is your address?
    *kayrâng-giy kajâng kâray ray?*    ཁྱེད་རང་གི་ཁ་བྱང་ག་རེ་རེད།

## Some Useful Words

| | | |
|---|---|---|
| ancient | *na ngâmo* | གནའ་སྔ་མོ |
| archaeological | *na-ngola tâgpay rignay* | གནའ་རྫོགས་ལ་བརྟགས་པའི་རིགས་གནས |
| building | *khâng-pa* | ཁང་པ |
| gardens | *dhumra* | ལྡུམ་ར |
| market | *trom* | ཁྲོམ |
| monument | *drensö-ten* | དྲན་གསོའི་རྟེན |
| mosque | *kache lha-khâng* | ཁ་ཆེའི་ལྷ་ཁང |
| old city | *dronkhay nyingpa* | གྲོང་ཁྱེར་རྙིང་པ |
| palace | *phodâng* | ཕོ་བྲང |
| statues | *dâku* | འདྲ་སྐུ |
| temple | *lha-khâng* | ལྷ་ཁང |
| university | *tsug-lak lobda* | གཙུག་ལག་སློབ་གྲྭ |

## *Visiting Temples*

Buddhism began to flourish in Tibet in the 7th century AD. There are many monasteries, nunneries, shrines and prayer flags, and inside people's houses you will see altars. In the streets you will see monks, nuns, and other local people walking around temples, saying prayers, lighting butter lamps and incense, and turning prayer wheels to show their spiritual devotion. Throughout the year there are many religious festivals.

**AROUND TOWN**

If you want to address a monk or a nun and you don't know their name, you can call monks *kusho-la* and nuns *ani-la*. Other titles for people associated with Buddhism are:

| | | |
|---|---|---|
| abbot | *khenpo* | མཁན་པོ |
| lama (teacher) | *lama* | བླ་མ |
| layperson | *kyâ-wo* | སྐྱ་བོ |
| monastic disciplinary | *gay-kö* | དགེ་སྐོས |
| student | *gay-toog/lob-ma* | དགེ་ཕྲུག / སློབ་མ |
| shrine keeper | *könyay* | བསྙེན་གཉེར |
| teacher | *genla* | རྒན་ལགས |

## Some Useful Phrases
What is that ... called?
... *phâgiy ming-la kâray ray?* ཕ་གིའི་མིང་ལ་ག་རེ་རེད

| | | |
|---|---|---|
| monastery | *gönpa* | དགོན་པ་ |
| nunnery | *ani gönpa* | ཨ་ནི་དགོན་པ་ |
| shrine | *lha-khâng* | ལྷ་ཁང་ |

When does it open/close?
  *kâdu go chay/gyâb-kiy ray?* ག་དུས་སྒོ་ཕྱེ་/བརྒྱབ་ཀྱི་རེད།

Am I allowed to go in (the temple)?
  *gönpay nâng dro chokiy rebay?* དགོན་པའི་ནང་འགྲོ་ཆོག་གི་རེད་པས།

Am I allowed to go upstairs?
  *toh-ga dro chokiy rebay?* ཐོག་ཁར་འགྲོ་ཆོག་གི་རེད་པས།

How many monks/nuns are there?
  *tâpa/âni kâtsay yawray?* གྲྭ་པ་/ཨ་ནི་ག་ཚོད་ཡོད་རེད།

I'd like to meet the abbot.
  *nga khenpo jel-dö yö* ང་མཁན་པོ་དང་མཇལ་འདོད་ཡོད།

May I offer ...?
  *...-chig bül-na digiy rebay?* ...ཅིག་ཕུལ་ན་འགྲིག་གི་རེད་པས།
    incense   *pö*   སྤོས་
    a butter lamp   *chömay*   མཆོད་མེ

Can I sit here for a while?
  *day te-tsi dayna digiy rebay?* འདིར་ཏོག་ཙམ་བསྡད་ན་འགྲིག་གི་རེད་པས།

Please say a prayer for me.
  *nga-la mönlâm kyön ronâng* ང་ལ་སྨོན་ལམ་བཏོན་རོགས་གནང་།

How far is Sera Monastery from here?
  *dinay sera gönpa tâ ring-lö yawray?* འདི་ནས་སེ་ར་དགོན་པ་བར་ཐག་རིང་ལོས་ཡོད་རེད།

I'd like to learn about
meditation.
*nga gom châng-dö yö*    ང་སྒོམ་སྦྱང་འདོད་ཡོད།

## Useful Words

| | | |
|---|---|---|
| altar | *chösom* | མཆོད་གསོམ་ |
| assembly hall | *tsog-khâng* | ཚོགས་ཁང་ |
| bell | *dilbu* | དྲིལ་བུ་ |
| Buddha | *sangye* | སངས་རྒྱས་ |
| circumambulation | *kora* | སྐོར་བ་ |
| cymbal | *boog-chel* | སྦུག་ཆལ་ |
| drum | *nga* | རྔ་ |
| gods/goddesses | *lhâ/lhâmo* | ལྷ་/ལྷ་མོ་ |

AROUND TOWN

| | | |
|---|---|---|
| His Holiness the Dalai Lama | *yeshin norbu* | ཡིད་བཞིན་ནོར་བུ |
| karma | *lay* | ལས |
| meditate | *gom* | སྒོམ |
| offering | *chöpa* | མཆོད་པ |
| prayer wheel | *mâni khorlo* | མ་ཎི་འཁོར་ལོ |
| prostrate | *châg-tsal* | ཕྱག་འཚལ |
| reincarnation | *kyewa nga-chi* | སྐྱེ་བ་སྔ་ཕྱི |
| reliquary | *chöten* | མཆོད་རྟེན |
| rosary | *tren-ngâ* | ཕྲེང་བ |
| scarf | *kâtâg* | ཁ་བཏགས |
| shrine | *lhakhâng* | ལྷ་ཁང |
| spiritual dance | *châm* | འཆམ |
| trumpet (small) | *gyâling* | རྒྱ་གླིང |
| trumpet (big) | *dung-chen* | དུང་ཆེན |
| vase | *bum-pa* | བུམ་པ |
| virtue | *gaywa* | དགེ་བ |
| non-virtue | *mi-gaywa* | མི་དགེ་བ |

## Entertainment

What is there to do in the evenings?

    *gönda kâray cheyak yawray?*    དགོང་དག་ག་རེ་བྱེད་ཡག་ཡོད་རེད

Are there any discos?

    *disiko yaw rebay?*    ཌི་སི་ཀོ་ཡོད་རེད་པས

Are there places where you can hear local music?

    *yümiy rolja nyensa yaw rebay?*    ཡུལ་མིའི་རོལ་ཆ་ཉན་ས་ཡོད་རེད་པས

How much is it to get in?
*dzula kâtsay nay-kiy ray?* རྡང་ལ་འཛུལ་བླ་ག་ཚོད་གནང་གི་རེད།

## Some Useful Words

| | | |
|---|---|---|
| cinema | *log-nyen* | གློག་བརྙན |
| concert | *roshe tro-tön* | རོལ་གཞས་སྒྲོ་སྟོན |
| nightclub/disco | *tsen-mo to-kyi* | མཚན་མོ་སྒྲོ་ཀྱིད |
| theatre | *trâbton-khâng* | བཁབ་སྟོན་ཁང |

## *Signs*

| | |
|---|---|
| DANGER | ཉེན་ཁ |
| ENTRANCE | འཛུལ་ས |
| EXIT | དོན་ས |
| STOP | ཁ་བཀག |
| OPEN | སྒོ་ཕྱེ |
| CLOSED | སྒོ་བརྒྱབ |
| NO PHOTOGRAPHS | པར་བརྒྱབ་མི་ཆོག |
| NO SMOKING | ཐ་མག་འཐེན་མི་ཆོག |
| TOILETS | གསང་སྤྱོད |

## *Paperwork*

| | | |
|---|---|---|
| name | *ming* | མིང |
| address | *kajâng* | ཁ་བྱང |
| date of birth | *kyetse* | སྐྱེས་ཚེས |

| | | |
|---|---|---|
| place of birth | *kye-yül* | སྐྱེས་ཡུལ་ |
| age | *lo* | ལོ་ |
| sex | *phomo kâng-yin* | ཕོ་མོ་གང་ཡིན་ |
| male | *pho* | ཕོ་ |
| female | *mo* | མོ་ |
| marital status | *châng-sa gyâb yö may* | ཆང་ས་བརྒྱབ་ཡོད་མེད་ |
| nationality | *lung-pa* | ལུང་པ་ |
| religion | *chö-lug* | ཆོས་ལུགས་ |
| reason for travel | *takor droyak gyutsen* | བསྐོར་འགྲོ་ཡག་རྒྱུ་མཚན་ |
| profession | *tsotâb* | འཚོ་ཐབས་ |
| passport | *chi-thön lâg-teb* | ཕྱིར་ཐོན་ལག་དེབ་ |
| passport number | *chi-thön lâg-teb âng* | ཕྱིར་ཐོན་ལག་དེབ་ཨང་གྲངས་ |
| visa | *zü-shug cho-chen/visa* | འཇུག་བཞག་ཆོག་མཆན།/ཝི་ཛ་ |
| birth certificate | *kyetse lâkay* | སྐྱེས་ཚེས་ལག་ཁྱེར་ |
| border | *sa-tsâm* | ས་མཚམས་ |
| car owner's title | *mota dâgpo ming* | མོ་ཊའི་བདག་པོའི་མིང་ |
| car registration | *motay tebkyel* | མོ་ཊའི་དེབ་སྐྱེལ་ |
| customs | *gâgo* | འགག་སྒོ་ |
| driver's licence | *mota ton-yagi lâkay* | མོ་ཊ་གཏོང་ཡ་གི་ལག་ཁྱེར་ |
| identification | *ngotö lâkay* | ངོ་སྤྲོད་ལག་ཁྱེར་ |
| immigration | *gyâkhâb shendu shi-châgpa* | རྒྱལ་ཁབ་གཞན་དུ་གནས་ཆགས་པ་ |
| tourist card | *tâkor lâkay* | བསྐོར་ལག་ཁྱེར་ |

# In the Country

One of the great delights of this country is its impressive scenery.
This chapter will help you with asking directions, asking about
flora, fauna and the general scenery, and with most of your basic
trekking needs.

## Weather

What's the weather like?
*namshi kan-day du?* གནམ་གཤིས་གང་འདྲས་འདུག

The weather is ... *dering namshi ... du* དེ་རིང་གནམ་གཤིས་ ...... འདུག
today.

Will it be ... *sanyin ... yaw rebay?* སང་ཉིན་གནམ་གཤིས་ ......
tomorrow? ཡོད་རེད་པས།

| | | |
|---|---|---|
| cold | *trang-mo* | གྲང་མོ |
| hot (very) | *tsha-po (shetah)* | ཚ་པོ (ཞེ་དྲགས) |
| windy | *lhag-pa tsha-po* | རླུང་པ་ཚ་པོ |

It is cloudy today.
*tering nam thib sha* དེ་རིང་གནམ་འཐིབ་ཤག
It is humid today.
*sha-tshen chenpo du* དེ་རིང་ཤ་ཚན་ཆེན་པོ་འདུག

It is raining today.
  *tering charpa bab-kiy ray*  དེ་རིང་ཆར་པ་བབས་ཀྱི་རེད།
It is snowing today.
  *tering gang bab-kiy ray*  དེ་རིང་གངས་བབས་ཀྱི་རེད།

## Some Useful Words

| | | |
|---|---|---|
| cloud | *tinpâ* | སྤྲིན་པ |
| dry season | *charpa konpo* | ཆར་པ་དགོན་པོ |
| | (lit: scarce rain) | |
| earth | *sa* | ས |
| fog | *mug-pâ* | སྨུག་པ |
| frost | *say/silpa/bamo* | སད/ཟིལབ/བམོ |
| ice | *kyag-pâ* | བཁྱགས་པ |
| mud | *dham-pag* | འདམ་པག |
| rain | *charpa* | ཆར་པ |
| rainy season | *char-du* | ཆར་དུས |
| snow | *gâng* | གངས |
| storm | *nam tshub-po* | གནམ་ཚུབས་བསཔོ |
| sun | *nyima* | ཉི་མ |
| thunderstorm | *tag-chàr* | འབྲུག་ཆར |
| weather | *nâmshi* | གནམ་གཤིས. |
| wind | *lhung* | རླུང |

## Seasons

| | | |
|---|---|---|
| spring | *chika* | དཔྱིད་ཀ |
| summer | *yarga* | དབྱར་ཁ |
| autumn | *tonka* | སྟོན་ཁ |
| winter | *gun-ga* | དགུན་ཁ |

## *Trekking*

Once you get off the main roads of Tibet, there is nothing in the way of support services, and very little in the way of accommodation and food. You'll also find that you'll have to use Tibetan to get by, as few people will understand English. Along the way you may be able to buy grain and other items of food from villagers, and on some trekking routes they may also allow you to stay in their homes.

### Arranging Transport

| | | |
|---|---|---|
| I want to rent a ... | *nga ... chig laygoyö* | ང་་་གཅིག་གླ་དགོས་ཡོད། |
| horse | *ta* | རྟ་ |
| donkey | *phung-gu* | ཕོང་གུ |

| | | |
|---|---|---|
| How much does it cost for each ...? | *... rayray-lâ laja kâtso ray?* | ་་་རེ་རེ་ལ་གླ་ཆ་ག་ཚོད་རེད། |
| day | *nyima* | ཉི་མ་ |
| week | *sa-khaw* | གཟའ་འཁོར་ |

Do I need a guide?<br>
*lâmgyu chay-khen gaw-kiy rebay?*     ལམ་རྒྱུས་བྱེད་མཁན་དགོས་ཀྱི་རེད་པས།

| | | |
|---|---|---|
| I need (a) ... | *nga ... chig gaw* | ང་ ··· གཅིག་དགོས། |
| guide | *lâmgyu chay-khen* | ལམ་རྒྱུས་བྱེད་མཁན། |
| porter | *dobo kay-ngen* | དོ་པོ་བཀུར་མཁན། |
| pack animal | *kaymâ* | ཁལ་མ། |

Can I get there on foot ?
*phâgay gompa gyab-nay leb*  ཕ་གིར་གོམ་པ་བརྒྱབ་ནས་སླེབས་ཐུབ་ཀྱི་རེད་པས།
*thub-kiy rebay?*

Can I get there on horseback?
*phâgay ta shön-nay leb*  ཕ་གིར་ད་འཆོན་ནས་སླེབས་ཐུབ་ཀྱི་རེད་པས།
*thub-kiy rebay?*

## Directions

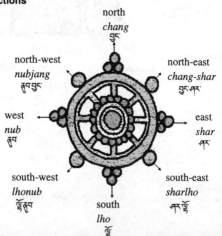

north
*chang*
བྱང་

north-west
*nubjang*
ནུབ་བྱང་

north-east
*chang-shar*
བྱང་ཤར་

west
*nub*
ནུབ་

east
*shar*
ཤར་

south-west
*lhonub*
ལྷོ་ནུབ་

south-east
*sharlho*
ཤར་ལྷོ་

south
*lho*
ལྷོ་

| Is this the trail/road to ...? | diy ... droya-kiy lang-ga rebay? | འདི་ ── འགྲོ་ཡས་ཀྱི་ལམ་ག ་རེད་པས། |
|---|---|---|
| Samye | samye | བསམ་ཡས། |
| Tsetang | tshedang | རྩེད་ཐང་། |
| Mt Kailash | gan rimpoche | གངས་རིན་པོ་ཆེ། |
| Drigung | drigung | འབྲི་གུང་། |

| Which way to ...? | ... droya-kiy lam kapar? | ── འགྲོ་ཡས་གི་ལམ་ག་པར། |
|---|---|---|

| downwards | maa | མར་ |
| upwards | yaa | ཡར་ |
| left | yon | གཡོན་ |
| right | yeh | གཡས་ |
| this side | di-chog | འདི་ཕྱོགས་ |
| that side | pha-chog | ཕ་ཕྱོགས་ |
| level/flat | ko nyom-po | བཀོལ་སྙོམ་པོ་ |
| (steep) uphill | gyen (sarbo) | གྱེན་ (ཟར་པོ) |
| (steep) downhill | tu (sarbo) | ཐུར་ (ཟར་པོ) |
| straight ahead | sha-gyak/kha-tu | ཤར་རྒྱག/ཁ་ཐུག |

## Distances

Along the motor roads in Tibet, distance is typically cited in *doban*, the road repair stations which can be seen every 10 km whilst travelling along the roads.

How many doban is it to
Saga district?
  *saga dzong bâdo doban kâtso yawray?*

ས་སྐ་རྫོང་བར་དུ་དོབ་སྐྱང་ག་ཚོད་ཡོད་རེད།

Other standard units to measure distance are:

| kilometre | kilometre/jili | ཀི་ལོ་མེ་ཏར་/ཇི་ལི |
| metre | metre/jidri | མེ་ཏར་/ཇི་ཏྲི |

## On the Trail

| What is the name of that ...? | ... phâgiy minglâ karay ray? | ...... ཕ་གིའི་མིང་ལ་ག་རེ་རེད། |
| bridge | sambâ | ཟམ་པ |
| lake | tsho | མཚོ |
| monastery | gombâ | དགོན་པ |
| pass | la | ལ |
| river | dzangbo/chu | གཙང་པོ་/ཆུ |
| village | lugbâ/thronsay | ལུང་པ/གྲོང་གསེབ |

What is the next village on
the trail?

| (going uphill) | dinay ya chin-nâ tang-go lungbâ karay lebgiy-ray? | འདི་ནས་ཡར་ཕྱིན་ན་དང་པོ་ ལུང་པ་ག་རེ་སླེབས་ཀྱི་རེད། |
| (going downhill) | dinay ma chin-nâ tang-go lungbâ karay lebgiy-ray? | འདི་ནས་མར་ཕྱིན་ན་དང་པོ་ ལུང་པ་ག་རེ་སླེབས་ཀྱི་རེད། |

Will we reach (Samye)
before dark?

*sa marup gawnlâ (samye-lâ)* ས་མ་རུབ་གོང་ལ་བསམ་ཡས་ལ་སླེབས་ཀྱི་རེད་པས།
*lebgiy-rebay?*

| How many ... to (Samye)? | (samye) bâdo ... kâdzay gogiyray? | (བསམ་ཡས)་བར་དུ་ ...... ག་ཚོད་དགོས་ཀྱི་རེད། |

| hours | chutsö | ཆུ་ཚོད་ |
| days | nyimâ | ཉིནལ |

| Is the trail ...? | lang-ga ... dugay? | ལམ་ག ------ འདུག་གས། |
| bad | dugcha | སྡུག་ཆགས། |
| good | yagpo | ཡག་པོ |
| narrow | togbo | དོག་པ |
| safe | ten-po | བརྟནཔོ |
| steep (uphill) | gyen sarbo | གྱེན་ཟར་པོ |
| steep (downhill) | tu sarbo | ཐུར་ཟར་པོ |
| uphill | gyen | གྱེན |
| downhill | tu | ཐུར |
| wide | gya chembo | རྒྱ་ཆེན་པོ |

I have to rest.

   *nga ngay-so gyab gokiy-du*    ང་ངལ་གསོ་བརྒྱབ་དགོས་ཀྱི་འདུག

I have to urinate/defecate.

   *nga chinpa/tsok-pa tang gokiy du*   ང་གཅིན་པ/བཙོག་པ་གཏང་དགོས་ཀྱི་འདུག

## Finding Somewhere to Stay

We will stop here for the
night.

   *togong ngantso day daygiy-yin*   དགོང་དག་ཚོ་འདིར་སྡོད་ཀྱི་ཡིན།

Are there any other areas to
stay apart from here?

   *diy membay lungbâ shenda*   འདི་མིན་པའི་ལུང་པ་གཞན་དག་ལ་སྡོད་ས
   *dösa dugay?*   འདུག་གས།

Can we get accommodation
at ...?
    *... lâ naydzang râgiy-rebay?*   ལ་གནས་ཚང་རག་གི་རེད་པས།

If you are invited to stay in a villager's house, it would be a good
idea to leave a small 'thank you' gift.

Do we have to pay to sleep in
your house?
    *kay-rangiy khang-par nela*   ཁྱེད་རང་གི་ཁང་པར་གནས་ན་གླ་སྤྲད་དགོས་རེད་པས།
    *dray go-rebay?*
Can we stay here tonight?
    *ngantso togong day daynâ*   ང་ཚོ་དགོང་འདིར་བསྡད་ན་འགྲིག་གི་རེད་པས།
    *digiy-rebay?*

## Food

Is there a restaurant?
    *sa-khang dugay?*   ཟ་ཁང་འདུག་གས།
Please make a meal for us
tonight.
    *togong kala chig sönandâ*   དོ་དགོང་ཁ་ལག་གཅིག་བཟོ་གནང་དང་།
Please make (boiled) potatoes
and tea.
    *shawgaw (chu-tso) tang cha*   ཞོག་ཁོག་(ཆུ་བཙོས་)དང་ཇ་བཟོ་རོགས་གནང་།
    *söronang*
Can one get food in that
village/place?
    *lungbâ day kala râ-giyray?*   ལུང་པ་ཕྱིར་ཁ་ལག་རག་གི་རེད་པས།
I'll pay you.
    *ngay laja draygi-yin*   ངས་གླ་ཆ་སྤྲད་གི་ཡིན།

Where is water?
*chu kaba yawray?* ཆུ་ག་པར་ཡོད་རེད།

Do you have any ... ... *dzon-ya yöbay?* ........ བཙོང་ཡག་ཡོད་པས།
to sell (us)?

| | | |
|---|---|---|
| parched barley flour | *tshambâ* | ཙམ་པ |
| flour | *thrushi* | གྲོ་ཞིབ |
| meat | *sha* | ཤ |
| potatoes | *shawgaw* | ཞོག་ཁོག |
| radish | *lâbu* | ལ་ཕུག |
| rice | *dray* | འབྲས |
| turnip | *nyungmâ* | ཉུང་མ |

Please lend me a ... *nga .. chig ya-nandâ* ང་ལ་ ........ གཅིག་གཡར་གནང་དང་།

| | | |
|---|---|---|
| ladle | *gyaw* | སྐྱོག |
| pot | *hayân/nöchay* | ཧ་ཡང་/སྣོད་ཆས |

## Some Useful Phrases

Is there firewood and water
here?
*day chu dâ mayshing dugay?* འདིར་ཆུ་དང་མེ་ཤིང་འདུག་གས།
I'm lost.
*ngay lang-ga ha kugiymindu* ངས་ལམ་ག་ཧ་གོ་གི་མིན་འདུག
Please help me.
*nga raw nandâ* ང་ལ་རོགས་གནང་དང་།
Where are you going?
*kaba payga?* ག་པར་ཕེབས་ག
Where are you coming from?
*kânay payba?* ག་ནས་ཕེབས་པ

Do we have to ask
permission from the leader?
*ganlâ nyesang shugo-rebay?*  ཀུན་ལགས་ལ་སྐུན་ཤེན་ཤུ་དགོས་རེད་པས།
Where is the leader?
*ganlâ kaba?*  ཀུན་ལགས་ག་པ།

## Animals & Birds

What's that animal called?
*sem-chen phâgiy ming-lâ karay*  སེམས་ཅན་ཕ་གིའི་མིང་ལ་ག་རེ་ཟ
*sa?*

| bird | cha/chi-u | བྱ་/བྱིའུ་ |
| camel | nga-mong | རྔ་མོང་ |
| cat | shimi | ཞི་མི་ |
| chicken | cha-day | བྱ་དེ་ |
| cow | bâ-chug | བ་ཕྱུགས་ |
| crocodile | chu-sin | ཆུ་སྲིན་ |
| dog | kyi | ཁྱི་ |

| | | |
|---|---|---|
| domestic animal | *go-chug* | ཁྱིམ་ཕྱུགས་ |
| donkey | *bon-gu* | བོང་བུ་ |
| fish | *nya* | ཉ་ |
| frog | *bag-pa* | སྦལ་པ་ |
| goat | *ra* | ར་ |
| horse | *ta* | རྟ་ |
| lizard | *tsang-pa kharel* | རྩང་པ་ཁ་རལ་ |
| monkey | *pi-u* | སྤྲེའུ་ |
| ox | *lan-gok* | གླང་གོག་ |
| pig | *phag-pa* | ཕག་པ་ |
| rooster | *cha-pho* | བྱ་ཕོ་ |
| sheep | *lug* | ལུག་ |
| snake | *drul* | སྦྲུལ་ |
| spider | *dhom-thag* | སྡོམ་ཐག་ |
| toad | *bag-pa rig* | སྦལ་པ་རིགས་ |
| turtle | *ru-bal* | རུས་སྦལ་ |
| wild animal | *ridag/nag-nay sogchag* | རི་དྭགས་/ ནགས་གནས་སྲོག་ཆགས་ |

## Insects

| | | |
|---|---|---|
| ant | *tog-ma* | གྲོག་མ་ |
| butterfly | *chem chem ma/ chema-leb* | ཅེམ་ཅེམ་མ་/ཕྱེ་མ་ལེབ་ |
| cockroach | *shombu* | ཤོམ་བུ་ |
| fly | *drang-bu* | སྦྲང་བུ་ |
| leech | *pay-pa/bu bay-bay* | པད་པ་/འབུ་སྦལ་སྦལ་ |

| lice | *shig* | ཤིག |
| mosquito | *du-drang* | དུག་སྦྲང་ |

## Plants

What's that plant called?
*tsi-shing phâgiy ming-lâ*  ཙི་ཤིང་ཕ་གིའི་མིང་ལ་ག་རེ་ཟ
*karay sa?*

| cactus | *lhu-shing* | ཀླུ་ཤིང་ |
| flower | *metog* | མེ་ཏོག |
| leaf | *loma* | ལོ་མ |
| palm tree | *shing tala* | ཤིང་ཏ་ལ |
| stick | *gyuk-pa* | རྒྱུག་པ |
| sugar cane | *bur-shing* | བུར་ཤིང་ |
| tree | *shing-tong* | ཤིང་སྟོང་ |

## Camping

Am I allowed to camp here?
*day gur gyab chogiy rebay?*  འདིར་གུར་བརྒྱབ་ཆོག་གི་རེད་པས།
Is there a campsite nearby?
*diy-pa gur gyab-sa yaw rebay?*  འདི་གར་གུར་བརྒྱབ་ས་ཡོད་རེད་པས།
I want to hire a tent.
*nga gur-chig yar gaw yo*  ང་གུར་གཅིག་གཡར་དགོས་ཡོད།
It is waterproof?
*chu kag thub-kiy ray?*  ཆུ་བཀག་ཐུབ་ཀྱི་རེད།

| backpack | *gyâ-phay* | རྒྱབ་ཕད་ |
| can opener | *chag-tin ka cheyak* | ལྕགས་ཏིན་ཁ་ཕྱེ་བྱེད་ལག |
| compass | *chog ta-gyu khorlo* | ཕྱོགས་བལྟ་རྒྱུ་འཁོར་ལོ |

| | | |
|---|---|---|
| crampons | *ri tang kadung dzeg-che chag gug-gug shig* | རི་དང་ཀ་དུང་འཛེག་ཆེད། ལྕགས་གུག་གུག་ཅིག |
| firewood | *me-shing* | མེ་ཤིང་ |
| gas cartridge | *du-lhang lug-no* | དུག་ལྷང་ལུགས་སྟོན་ |
| ice axe | *kyag-pa chogyu taray* | བཀྱགས་པ་གཅོག་རྒྱུའི་སྟ་རེ་ |
| mattress | *den* | གདན་ |
| penknife | *teb-di* | སྟེབ་གྲི་ |
| rope | *thag-pa* | ཐག་པ་ |
| tent | *gur* | གུར་ |
| tent pegs | *phur-pâ* | ཕུར་པ་ |
| torch (flashlight) | *log-shu/bijili* | གློག་བཤུ/བི་ཇི་ལི་ |
| sleeping bag | *pho-keb* | ཕོ་འབེབས་ |
| stove | *thâb* | ཐབ་ |
| water bottle | *chulug-no shetam* | ཆུ་ལུག་སྟོན་ཤེལ་དམ་ |

## Some Useful Words

| | | |
|---|---|---|
| agriculture | *shinglay* | ཞིང་ལས་ |
| beach | *tsho-dam jetang* | མཚོ་འགྲམ་བྱེ་ཐང་ |
| bridge | *sampa* | ཟམ་པ་ |
| cave | *dag-phug* | བྲག་ཕུག |
| city | *drong-kay* | གྲོང་ཁྱེར་ |
| country person | *drong-seb mi* | གྲོང་གསེབ་མི་ |
| desert | *je-tang* | བྱེ་ཐང་ |
| earthquake | *sa-yom* | ས་ཡོམ་ |
| farm | *shing-ga* | ཞིང་ཁ་ |

| | | |
|---|---|---|
| forest | *shing-nag* | ཤིང་ནགས |
| grassy plains | *tsaka* | རྩ་ཁ |
| harbour | *dru-khang* | གྲུ་ཁང |
| (lit: boat station) | | |
| high plateau | *sa thopo tang-chen* | ས་མཐོ་པོའི་ཐང་ཆེན |
| hill | *ri* | རི |
| hot spring | *chu-tshen* | ཆུ་ཚན |
| island | *tsho-ling* | མཚོ་གླིང |
| jungle | *shing-nag* | ཤིང་ནགས |
| lake | *tsho* | མཚོ |
| landslide | *saru* | ས་རུད |
| mountain | *ri* | རི |
| mountain range | *ri-gyu* | རི་རྒྱུད |
| national park | *mimang ling-ga* | མི་དམངས་གླིང་ག |
| ocean | *gyam-tsho* | རྒྱ་མཚོ |
| river | *tsang-po* | གཙང་པོ |
| scenery | *yu-jong* | ཡུལ་ལྗོངས |
| village | *drong-seb* | གྲོང་གསེབ |
| waterfall | *bab-chu* | འབབ་ཆུ |

# Food

Most of the restaurants in Lhasa and Tibet's other towns serve Chinese-type dishes, either noodles (*gyâdu*) or stir-fried vegetable dishes (*tshay*). It's also possible to find some restaurants that serve the traditional Tibetan steamed meat dumpling (*momo*), and in Lhasa, some restaurants serve Western food such as fried potatoes and stew.

| restaurant | *sa-khang* | ཟ་ཁང་ |
| cheap restaurant | *sa-khang khepo* | ཟ་ཁང་ཁེ་པོ་ |
| food stall | *khala nyosa* | ཁ་ལག་ཉོ་ས་ |
| grocery store | *sa-chay tshong-khang* | ཟ་བཅའི་ཚོང་ཁང་ |
| delicatessen | *tso sinpay khala migsel nyosa* | བཙོས་ཟིན་པའི་ཁ་ལག་དམིགས་བསལ་ཉོ་ས་ |
| breakfast | *shawgay khala* | ཞོགས་སྐད་ཁ་ལག་ |
| lunch | *nyin-gung khala* | ཉིན་གུང་ཁ་ལག་ |
| dinner | *gawnda khala* | དགོང་དག་ཁ་ལག་ |

## At the Restaurant

A table for ... please.
> *...-la chog-tse chig nang ro*　ༀ་ཆོག་ཙེ་གཅིག་གནང་རོགས།

Can I see the menu please?
> *nga la khala-giy tho ton-ro nang?*　ང་ལ་ཁ་ལག་གི་ཐོ་སྟོན་རོགས་གནང་།

Do you have a menu in English?
> *injiy-kay-tho khala-giy tho yaw bay?*　དབྱིན་ཇི་སྐད་ཐོག་ཁ་ལག་གི་ཐོ་ཡོད་པས།

What is this/that?
> *diy/phâgiy karay ray?*　འདི་/ཕ་གི་ག་རེ་རེད།

What do you recommend?
> *kayrang-kiy chayna, karay yâgi ray?*　ཁྱེད་རང་གིས་བྱེད་ན་ག་རེ་ཡག་གི་རེད།

Please bring me ...
> *... chig day ro nang*　ང་ལ་གཅིག་སྟེར་རོགས་གནང་།

I'd like the set lunch please.
> *nga la nyin-gung solton nang ro*　ང་ལ་ཉིན་གུང་གསོལ་སྟོན་གནང་རོགས།

What does it include?
> *tay nang-la khala garay garay yawray?*　དེའི་ནང་ལ་ཁ་ལག་ག་རེ་ག་རེ་ཡོད་རེད།

Not too spicy, please.
> *man-na shayda ma-gyab ro nang*　སྨན་སྣ་ཤེ་དགས་མ་བརྒྱབ་རོགས་གནང་།

Another ... please. (I want more ...)
> *datung ... chig nang ro*　ད་དུང་གཞན་དག་ༀ་གཅིག་གནང་རོགས།

Nothing more?
> *ta drig-song?*　ད་འགྲིགས་སོང་།

Anything else?
*shenda gay gawbay?*   གཞན་དག་གས་དགོས་པས།

The meal was delicious.
*khala shimbu shedra chung*   ཁ་ལག་ཞིམ་པོ་ཞེ་དྲགས་བྱུང་།

Please bring the bill.
*ngü dziy könda*   ཁ་ལག་གི་དངུལ་རྩིས་བསྐྱོན་དང་།

Is service included in the bill?
*ngü-dziy nang leka-la tsi yaw rebay?*   དངུལ་རྩིས་ནང་ལས་ཀ་ལ་རྩི་ཡོད་རེད་པས།

## Specialities

*momo*   མོག་མོག

   steamed meat dumplings

*chimay momo*   ཆེ་སྨན་མོག་མོག

   steamed 'yeast' meat dumplings

*hru jaudzâ*   ཧྲུལ་ཅོའི་ཙོ

   meat dumplings in soup

*khoday*   ཀོ་དེ

   fried meat dumplings

*thri momo/mentau*   གྲིའི་མོག་མོག / མན་ཏོ

   steamed bread

*sha palay*   ཤ་བལག་ལེབ

   fried pancake (bread) stuffed with meat

## Vegetarian

I don't eat meat.
*nga sha sâgi may*   ང་ཤ་ཟ་གི་མེད།

Do you have dishes without meat?
*sha maybay khala yawbay?*   ཤ་མེད་པའི་ཁ་ལག་ཡོད་པས།

## Complaints

This is not what I ordered.
  *diy ngay nga-bâday maray*    འདི་རས་མངགས་པ་དེ་མ་རེད།

This … doesn't taste good.
  *diy … shimbu mindu*    ……འདི་ཞིམ་པོ་མི་འདུག

| This … | *diy …* | ……འདི་ |
|---|---|---|
| is cold | *trâng-mo chagsha* | གྲང་མོ་ཆགས་ས་ལ་ས་ག |
| is rotten | *rüsha* | རུལ་ས་ག |
| isn't clean | *tsangmö mindu* | གཙང་མ་མི་འདུག |
| is dirty | *tsokbâ raysha* | བཙོག་པ་རེད་ས་ག |

| This is too … | *diy … ta-shag* | འདི་……དྲགས་ས་ག |
|---|---|---|
| sweet | *ngar* | མངར་ |
| hot | *tsa* | ཚ་ |
| cold | *trang* | གྲང་ |

## Cooking Methods

| baked | *drö-tsö* | རྟོད་བཙོས་ |
|---|---|---|
| barbecued | *chagtab gânla trâgpa* | ལྕགས་ཐབ་སྒང་ལ་བརྒྱགས་པ |
| boiled | *chu-tsö* | ཆུ་བཙོས་ |

| deep-fried | *num nâng ngö-pa* | སྣུམ་ནང་རྔོས་པ་ |
| fried | *ngö-pa* | བརྔོས་པ་ |
| grilled | *châgtâb nâng-la trâgpa* | ལྕགས་ཐབ་ནང་ལ་བསྒྲགས་པ་ |
| roasted | *me-tâg gyâb-pa* | མེ་བཀག་བརྒྱབ་པ་ |
| steamed | *lâng-tsö* | རྡང་བཙོས་ |
| stir-fried | *ngö-trug chenay tsöpa* | རྔོ་དཀྲུག་བྱེད་ནས་བཙོས་པ་ |

## Some Useful Words & Phrases

I am hungry.
  *nga dröko togiy du*        ང་གྲོད་ཁོག་ལྟོག་གི་འདུག
I am thirsty.
  *nga kha komgiy du*        ངའ་ཁ་སྐོམ་གྱི་འདུག

| ashtray | *thama dâbsa* | ཐ་མག་དབས་ |
| bill/check | *ngü-tsiy/ngü-zin* | དངུལ་ཚིས་/དངུལ་འཛིན་ |
| bowl | *phorpa* | ཕོར་པ་ |
| chopsticks | *kötse* | བཟོས་རྩེ་ |
| cold | *trâng-mo* | གྲང་མོ་ |
| cup (drinking tea) | *ka-yol/cha-phor* | དཀར་ཡོལ་/ཇ་ཕོར་ |
| drink (v) | *tung* | འཐུང་ |
| eat (v) | *sah* | ཟ་ |
| fork | *kâng-dra* | ཀང་གྲ་ |
| fresh | *söpa* | སོས་པ་ |
| glass | *gilasiy* | གྲི་ལ་སི་ |
| knife | *dri* | གྲི་ |
| mug | *mog* | མོག་ |
| napkin | *ka chiya-kiy shawray* | ཁ་ཕྱིས་ལ་ག་གི་ཤོག་རས་ |

| plate | ta-ba | ཐབ |
| ripe | min | སྨིན |
| set menu | sotön | གསོལ་སྟོན |
| spicy | mena mângpo | སྨན་སྣ་མང་པོ |
| spoon | tuma | ཐུར་མ |
| stale | nying-pa | རྙིང་པ |
| sweet | ngar-mo | མངར་མོ |
| teaspoon | tuma chung chung | ཐུར་མ་ཆུང་ཆུང |
| toothpick | so ngoya-kiy shing | སོ་རྙོག་ལྱག་གི་ཤིང |

## Breakfast

| ... eggs | gaw-ngâ ... | སྒོང |
|   hard-boiled | dhog-tsö | རྡོག་བཙོས |
|   soft-boiled | chay-tsö | ཆེད་བཙོས |
|   fried | ngöbâ | བཙོས་པ |
| omelette | gawn-dre ngöbâ | སྒོན་འབྲས་བཙོས་པ |
| bread | baleb | བག་ལེབ |
| toast | palay tragpâ | བག་ལེབ་གྲགས་པ |
| jam | shing-day mar/jam | ཤིང་འབྲས་མར/ཇེམ |
| porridge-type foods | thug-pa | ཐུག་པ |
| rice porridge | dray-du | འབྲས་ཐུག |

## At the Market

Do you have any ... to sell?
  *kayranglâ ... tsong-ya yöbay?* ཁྱེད་རང་ལ་...་འཚོང་ཡག་ཡོད་པས།

How much does the ... cost?
  *...-la gawn kâtsay ray?* ...་གོང་ག་ཚད་རེད།

I'll buy … kilos.
*ngay kilo … nyo-giy yin*   ངས་ཀི་ལོ་... ཉོ་གི་ཡིན།

## Grains

| | | |
|---|---|---|
| barley | *nay* | ནས |
| corn | *ah-shom* | ཨ་ཤོམ |
| buckwheat (sweet) | *gya-da* | གྱ་དྲ |
| popped barley | *nay-yö* | ནས་ཡོས |
| popped rice | *dray-yö* | འབྲས་ཡོས |
| rice | *dray* | འབྲས |

## Dairy Products

| | | |
|---|---|---|
| butter | *mar* | མར |
| cheese | *churâ* | ཕྱུ་ར |
| fresh cheese | *churâ söbâ* | ཕྱུ་ར་གསོལ་བ |
| dried cheese | *churâ gambo* | ཕྱུ་ར་སྐམ་པོ |
| cream | *tri* | ཁྲི |
| ice cream | *kyagpa ngarmo* | ཁྱགས་པ་མངར་མོ |
| milk | *oma* | འོ་མ |
| yoghurt | *sho* | ཞོ |

## Meat

| | | |
|---|---|---|
| beef | *lang-sha* | གླང་ཤ |
| boiled meat | *sha tsöbâ* | ཤ་བཙོས་པ |
| chicken | *cha-sha* | བྱ་ཤ |
| dried meat | *sha kambo* | ཤ་སྐམ་པོ |
| fish | *nya-sha* | ཉ་ཤ |
| lamb | *lug-sha* | ལུག་ཤ |
| pork | *phak-sha* | ཕག་ཤ |
| roast meat | *shap-tra* | ཤ་བསྲེག |
| yak meat | *tshag-sha/yak-sha* | གཡག་ཤ |

## Vegetables

| | | |
|---|---|---|
| beans | *trayma* | སྲན་མ |
| cabbage (Chinese-style) | *pay-tsay* | པད་ཚལ |
| carrot | *gawn lâbu* | སྐྱོང་ལ་ཕུག |
| cauliflower | *pool-gobi* | ཕུལ་གོ་བི |
| corn | *a-shom* | ཨ་ཤོམ |
| cucumber | *kang-ra/huang gâ* | གང་ར/ཀུང་ག |
| eggplant | *chay-dze* | ཚལ་ཨེ་ཚེ |
| green pepper | *solo ngom-bo* | སོ་ལོ་སྔོན་པོ |
| onion | *tsong* | ཙོང |
| peas | *trayma* | སྲན་མ |
| pickled radish | *sön lâbu* | སོན་ལ་ཕུག |
| potato | *shaw-gaw* | ཞོག་ཁོག |
| radish | *lâbu* | ལ་ཕུག |
| spinach | *po-tsay* | པོ་ཚལ |

| spring onion | tsong ngon-po | ཙོང་སྔོན་པོ |
| tomato | tomato | ཏོ་མ་ཏོ |
| turnip | nyung-mâ | ཉུང་མ |

## Condiments & Spices

| cardamom | sung-men | སུག་སྨེལ |
| caraway | go-nyö | གོ་སྙོད |
| chilli (ground) | siben | ཤི་པན |
| chilli (with water) | siben mân-du | ཤི་པན་དམར་པདུར |
| cinnamon | shing-tsa | ཤིང་ཚ |
| coriander | sona bendzo | བསོད་ནམས་པད་འབོལ |
| garlic | gokba | སྒོག་པ |
| ginger | gâmu | སྐ་སྨུག |
| mustard | yung-kar/paykang | ཡུངས་ཀར/པེ་གང |
| oil | num | སྣུམ |
| pepper | emâ | གའེར་མ |
| salt | tsa | ཚ |
| soy sauce | châng-yu | བྱང་ཡུལ |
| sugar | chayma-kara | བྱེ་མ་ཀ་ར |
| vinegar | tshu | ཚུར |

## Fruit & Nuts

| fruit | shing-tog | ཤིང་ཏོག |
| apple | ku-shu | ཀུ་ཤུ |
| apricot | ngâri khâmbu | མངའ་རིས་ཁམ་བུ |
| banana | kela | གི་ལ |
| berry | say-u | སེའུ |

| | | |
|---|---|---|
| grape | *chu gundrum* | ཆུ་རྒུན་འབྲུམ |
| lemon | *limbu* | ལིམ་བུ |
| mango | *shingdo-ahm* | ཤིང་ཏོག་ཨཱམ |
| orange/tangerine | *tsâlumâ* | ཚ་ལུམ |
| peanut | *ba-dam* | བ་དམ |
| pear | *li* | ལི |
| pomegranate | *sin-dru* | སེན་འབྲུ |
| rhubarb | *chuchu* | ཆུ་རྩི |
| walnut | *tarka* | སྟར་ཀ |

## Other Essentials

| | | |
|---|---|---|
| cake | *tenshi/kayk* | གོག/རྟེན་ཤིས |
| candy | *jiriy* | བྱི་རིལ |
| cookies | *kapsay/tenshi* | ཁབ་སེ |
| fried potatoes | *shawgaw ngöbâ* | ཞོག་ཁོག་རྔོས་པ |
| noodles | *gyâdu* | རྒྱ་ཐུག |
| pancakes | *khurâ* | ཁུར་ར |
| parched flour (usually barley) | *tsampa* | རྩམ་པ |
| powdered milk | *o-tsam* | འོ་ཚམ |
| soup | *thang* | ཐང |
| vermicelli (bean thread) | *phing* | ཕིང |

## *Drinks*
### Cold Drinks

| | | |
|---|---|---|
| beer (home brew) | *chang* | ཆང |

| beer (bottle) | *piju/beeyar* | པི་ཅུ/སྦི་ཡར་ |
| soda | *chu ngamo* | ཆུ་མངར་མོ་ |
| orange soda | *tsâ-lumay chu ngamo* | ཚ་ལུ་མའི་ཆུ་མངར་མོ་ |
| juice | *shintog khuwa* | ཤིང་ཏོག་ཁུ་བ་ |
| orange juice | *tsâ-lumay khuwa* | ཚ་ལུ་མའི་ཁུ་བ་ |
| liquor | *a-rak* | ཨ་རག |
| milk | *omâ* | འོ་མ་ |
| water | *chu* | ཆུ་ |
| boiled water | *chu khöma* | ཆུ་འཁོལ་མ་ |
| mineral water | *butog chu* | བུག་ཏོག་ཆུ་ |
| wine | *gundrum-kyi chang* | གུན་འབྲུམ་གྱི་ཆང་ |

## Hot Drinks

| coffee | *cha kabi/tsigcha* | ཇ་ཀོ་ཕི/ཚིག་ཇ་ |
| black coffee | *cha kabi oma maypa* | ཇ་ཀོ་ཕི་ཨོ་མ་མེད་པ་ |
| tea | *cha* | ཇ་ |
| black tea | *cha-tang* | ཇ་ཐང་ |
| Tibetan tea (tea with butter) | *pöja/cha suma* | བོད་ཇ/སྲུབ་མ་ |
| tea with sugar | *cha ngamo* | ཇ་མངར་མོ་ |
| Chinese-style tea | *chin-drang* | ཅིན་ཕྲང་ |

# Shopping

The best place to look for souvenirs in Tibet is the *Barkhor* in Lhasa (the circumambulation surrounding the *Jokhang* temple) which sells many trinkets such as prayer flags, prayer shawls and prayer wheels. There are carpet factories in Lhasa and Shigatse which produce carpets of an average quality. Some pharmaceutical items are hard to find even in Lhasa, including shaving cream, decent razor blades, mosquito repellent, tampons and contact lens cleaner.

Where is the nearest ...?
   ... *nyayshö kaba yawray?*     ཉེ་ཤོས་ག་པར་ཡོད་རེད།
How far is the ... from here?
   *diynay ... ta ringlö kâtsay*     འདི་ནས་ ... ཐག་རིང་ལོད་ག་ཚོད་ཡོད་རེད།
   *yawray?*

| | | |
|---|---|---|
| bank | *ngü khâng* | དངུལ་ཁང་ |
| bookshop | *teb tshong-khâng* | དེབ་ཚོང་ཁང་ |
| market | *trom* | ཁྲོམ |
| pharmacy | *men tshong-khâng* | སྨན་ཚོང་ཁང་ |
| camera shop | *par-khâng* | པར་ཁང་ |
| tailor | *tshem-buwa* | ཚེམས་བུ་ཁང་ |

| telegraph office | *tar tongsay lay-gung* | དར་གོང་རའི་ལས་ཁུངས |
| Tibetan rug store | *pö-kiy rumden tshong-khâng* | བོད་ཀྱི་རུམ་གདན་ཚོང་ཁང |

Where can I buy ...?
*... kaba nyo tugiy ray?* ····· ག་པར་ཉོ་ཐུབ་ཀྱི་རེད

### Bargaining

In Lhasa you shouldn't try bargaining in the department stores, but the individual merchants in the open markets and street stalls are almost always willing to haggle over the price.

It's too expensive.
*diy gong chay tra-sha* འདི་གོང་ཆེ་དྲགས་ཤག
What's your real price?
*gong ngaw-nay sundâ?* གོང་དངོས་གནས་གསུང་དང
I don't have much money.
*nga-la ngü shay-ta may* ང་ལ་དངུལ་ཞེ་དྲགས་མེད
Could you give me a discount?
*gong châg thupki rebay?* གོང་བཅག་ཐུབ་ཀྱི་རེད་པས
I'll give you ...
*ngay ... tay go* ངས་ ····· སྤྲད་གོ

## *Making a Purchase*

(Hey) Mr/Ms, please come
here.
    *genla, day pay-nâng*    ཀུན་ལགས། འདིར་ཕེབས་གནང་།

I would like to buy …
    *nga ... chig nyo-dö yo*    ང ᎏᎏ གཅིག་ཉོ་འདོད་ཡོད།

Do you have any ...
    *kayrang-la ... yawbay?*    ཁྱེད་རང་ལ ᎏᎏ ཡོད་པས།

I'm just looking.
    *nga tagâsi mig-tâgiyo*    ང་དགའ་སེ་མིག་བལྟ་གི་ཡོད།

Can you show me that?
    *chala phâgiy miy töndâ?*    ཙ་ལགས་ཕ་གི་མིག་སྟོན་དང་།

Not that one. This one.
    *phâgiy maray, diy ray*    ཕ་གི་མ་རེད། འདི་རེད།

Is this for sale?
    *diy tson-ya rebay?*    འདི་འཚོང་ཡག་རེད་པས།

How much is it?
    *gong gâtsay ray?*    གོང་ག་ཚད་རེད།

Please write down the price.
    *gong-tsay shugu gâng-la*    གོང་ཚད་ཤོག་གུ་གང་ལ་བྲིས་རོགས་གནང་།
    *driy-nandâ*

I'll buy this one.
    *nga diy nyo-giy yin*    ང་འདི་ཉོ་གི་ཡིན།

Do you accept credit cards?
    *ngu-tshâb lâgkye-thog rimpa*    དངུལ་ཚབ་ལག་ཁྱེར་ཐོག་རིན་པ་སྤྲོད་ན་འགྲིག
    *phüna digiy rebay?*    གི་རེད་པས།

What is this made of?
    *diy gyubjâ kâray ray?*    འདི་རྒྱུ་ཆ་ག་རེ་རེད།

Where does this come from?
    *diy lung-ba kânay thönbâ ray?*    འདི་ལུང་པ་ག་ནས་ཐོན་པ་རེད།

| Is this ...? | *diy ... rebay?* | འདི་ ···· རེད་པས། |
| amber | *pöshay* | སྤོས་ཤེལ |
| gold | *ser* | གསེར། |
| jade | *dzu/yângti* | ཧྥུལ/གཡང་ཏི |
| silver | *ngü* | དངུལ |
| turquoise | *yu* | གཡུ། |

| This is too ... | *diy ... ta-shâg* | འདི་ ···· དྲགས་ཤག |
| big | *chay* | ཆེ |
| small | *chung* | ཆུང་ |

I don't like this colour.
   *nga tshü-shi diyla gâbo mindu* ང་ཚོས་གཞི་འདི་ལ་དགའ་པོ་མིན་འདུག
Do you have another (colour)?
   *(tshü-shi) shenda yöbay?* ཚོས་གཞི་གཞན་དག་ཡོད་པས།

**You Might Hear**
There is none/We don't have
any.
   *kyo-nay yaw maray/* ཁྱོར་ནས་ཡོང་མ་རེད།/
   *nga tsor kyo-nay may* ང་ཚོར་ཁྱོར་ནས་མེད།
Which one?
   *ka-gi gaw?* ག་གི་དགོས།
This one?
   *diy gobay* འདི་དགོས་པས།

## Souvenirs

| amber | *pöshay* | སྤོས་ཤེལ |
| carpets | *rumden* | རུམ་གདན |

| | | |
|---|---|---|
| earrings | *âm-cho gyen* | འམ་ཚོག་རྒྱན་ |
| gold | *say* | གསེར་ |

| | | |
|---|---|---|
| handicraft | *lâgshay* | ལག་ཤེས་ |
| necklace | *kay-gyen* | སྐེ་རྒྱན་ |
| pottery | *dza-chay* | རྫ་ཆས་ |
| ring | *tsi-kok* | ཚིགས་ཞིབས་ |
| rug | *khâden* | ཁ་གདན་ |
| silver | *ngü* | དངུལ་ |
| turquoise | *yu* | གཡུ་ |

## Clothing

| | | |
|---|---|---|
| belt | *kayrâ* | སྐེད་རགས་ |
| blouse | *wâng-ju* | ཝོན་བྱུག་ |
| clothing | *tulog* | དུག་ལོག་ |
| coat | *tö-dung/kot* | སྟོད་གདུབ/ཀོཊ |
| dress | *chubâ* | ཕྱུ་པ་ |
| gloves | *lâg-shub* | ལག་ཤུབས་ |
| hat | *shamo* | ཞྭ་མོ་ |

| | | |
|---|---|---|
| jacket | tö-dung/jaket | སྟོད་གྱོན/ཇ་ཀེཊི |
| jeans | jiyn | འཇིན |
| jumper/pullover | balen/omosu tö-dung | སྦ་ལེན/ཨུ་མོ་སུའི་སྟོད་གྱོན |
| sandals | chapaliy | ཅ་པ་ལི |
| shirt | tö-dung/wâng-ju | སྟོད་གྱོན/ཕྱིན་འཇུག |
| shoes | lhâm-kok/jurdâ | ལྷམ་གོག/འཇུར་ད |
| shorts | gö-düng wog-dö/<br>haf pant | ཅ་ལག/གོས་གྱོན་ཝོག་དོ |
| skirt | may-yog | སྨད་གཡོག |
| socks | usu/omosulu | ཨུ་སུ/ཨུ་མོ་སུ |
| sweater | balen/osü tö-dung | སྦ་ལེན/ཨུ་སུའི་སྟོད་གྱོན |
| trousers | kudung | གོས་གྱོན |
| T-shirt | gong-may dudung<br>phuche | གོང་མེད་སྟོད་གྱོན་ཕུ་ཆེ |
| underwear | nâng-gyon haf pant | ནང་གོན་ཧ་པཎ |

Can I try it on?
    *tsöta-che kön-na digiy rebay?* ཚོད་བལྟ་ཆེད་གྱོན་ན་འགྲིག་གི་རེད་པས

It doesn't fit.
    *di tâgtâg ray mindu* འདི་ཏག་ཏག་རེད་གི་མི་འདུག

Can it be altered?
    *sochö gyâb thupki rebay?* བཟོ་བཅོས་རྒྱག་ཐུབ་ཀྱི་རེད་པས།

## Materials

| | | |
|---|---|---|
| corduroy | shurmâ | ཤུར་མ |
| cotton | ray | རས |
| felt | chingpâ | ཕྱིང་པ |
| leather | kowa | ཀོ་བ |

| nylon | *nilen* | ནི་ལེན་ |
| silk | *dru-dzi* | གྲུ་ཙི་ |
| velvet | *pumâ* | གྲུ་མ་ |
| wool | *bay* | བལ་ |

## Colours

| black | *nâgbo* | ནག་པོ་ |
| blue | *ngom-bo* | སྔོན་པོ་ |
| brown | *mar-mug/gya-mug* | དམར་སྨུག / རྒྱ་སྨུག |
| dark | *nâg-bo* | ནག་པོ་ |
| green | *jâng-gu* | ལྗང་ཁུ་ |
| light | *kya-wo* | སྐྱ་པོ་ |
| orange | *mâsay/li-hâng* | དམར་སེར / ལི་ཁྲ་ |
| pink | *sing-kya* | སིང་སྐྱ་ |
| purple | *ngo-mar/mu-man* | སྔོན་དམར / མུ་མན་ |
| red | *mah-bo* | དམར་པོ་ |
| white | *ka-bo* | དཀར་པོ་ |
| yellow | *say-bo* | སེར་པོ་ |

## Toiletries

| aspirin | *gomen aspirin* | མགོ་སྨན་ཨེ་སི་པི་རིན་ |
| baby's bottle | *pugu oma teyak shetâm* | གུ་གུ་པོ་ཨ་སྐྲ་ལྷག་ཤེལ་དམ་ |
| baby powder | *pugu sugpo juyâk pota* | ཕྲུག་གུའི་གཟུགས་པོ་བྱུག་ལྷག་པོ་ཏར་ |
| comb | *gyug-shay* | རྒྱུག་ཤས་ |
| condoms | *lig-shup* | བྲེག་ལྷབས་ |

| deodorant | ludi gokmen | ལུས་ལ་དྲི་བཟོག་སྨན |
| face cream | shasö | ཤ་གཤོལ |
| hairbrush | gyu-shay/pando | ཀྱུ་ལས/ཕྱག་མོ |
| hair dye | ta-tsö | སྐྲ་ཚོས |
| insect repellent | bu-dâng gokmen | འབུ་སྲང་བཟོག་སྨན |
| medicine | men | སྨན |
| moisturising cream | shâb-sö | ཤ་གཤོལ |
| razor | pudi | སྤུ་གྲི |
| sanitary napkins | tsâng-dray shugu | གཙང་སྦྲའི་ཤོག་གུ |
| shampoo | ta tru-yak shampu | སྐྲ་བཀྲུ་ལག་ཤམ་པུ |
| shaving cream | ahra shardu juyak men | ཨར་བཞར་དུ་སྦྱུག་ལགས་སྨན |
| soap | yi-tsi | ཨི་ཚི |
| sunblock cream | nyib-tâg gokmen | ཉི་བཟོག་བཟོག་སྨན |
| talcum powder | sugpor juyak potah | གཟུགས་པོར་སྦྱུག་ལགས་པ་ཏར |
| tampons | tâg-chö sinbay | ཁག་གཅོད་སྲིན་བལ |
| tissues | dhong chiyak shugu | གདོང་ཕྱིས་ལག་ཤོག་གུ |
| toilet paper | tsâng-dray shugu | གཙང་སྦྲའི་ཤོག་གུ |
| toothbrush | so-trü | སོ་ཁྲུ |
| toothpaste | somen | སོ་སྨན |
| water purification<br>  tablets | chu tsângma<br>  soyak men | ཆུ་གཙང་མ་བཟོས་ལགས་སྨན |

## Stationery & Publications

| book | teb | དེབ |
|   book in Tibetan | pökay teb | བོད་སྐད་དེབ |
|   book in English | injiykay teb | དབྱིན་ཇི་སྐད་དེབ |

| | | |
|---|---|---|
| dictionary | *tshing-dzö* | ཚིག་མཛོད་ |
| Tibetan-English dictionary | *phö-in tshing-dzö* | བོད་དབྱིན་ཚིག་མཛོད་ |
| exercise book | *jongdah ti-teb* | སྦྱོང་བདར་འབྲི་དེབ་ |
| envelope | *yigaw* | ཡིག་སྒྲོག་ |
| glue | *jârtsi* | སྦྱོར་ཚི་ |
| magazine | *tü-teb* | དུས་དེབ་ |
| map | *sâpta* | ས་བཀྲ་ |
| city map | *tongkye sâpta* | གྲོང་ཁྱེར་ས་བཀྲ་ |
| trekking map | *rilung droyakiy sâpta* | རི་ལུང་འགྲོ་ཡག་གི་ས་བཀྲ་ |
| newspaper | *tshâgba* | ཚགས་པར་ |
| newspaper in English | *injikay tshâgba* | དབྱིན་ཇི་སྐད་ཚགས་པར་ |
| notebook | *ti-teb* | འབྲི་དེབ་ |
| novel | *dung-teb/nâmthar* | སྒྲུང་དེབ་/རྣམ་ཐར་ |
| pad (letter writing) | *tânyig tisay teb* | གཏོང་ཡིག་འབྲི་སའི་དེབ་ |
| pen | *nyugu* | སྙུ་གུ་ |
| pencil | *shânyu* | ཞ་སྙུག་ |
| scissors | *jâmtse* | ཇེམ་ཚེ་ |
| writing paper | *ti-shog* | འབྲི་ཤོག་ |

## *Photography*

I'd like a film for this camera.

    *parchay diyla phing-sho chig gaw*    པར་ཆས་འདི་ལ་པར་ཤོག་གཅིག་དགོས།

How much is it for processing/developing?

    *phing-sho trüla kâtsay ray?*    པར་ཤོག་བཀྲུ་ལུ་གོང་ག་ཚད་རེད།

When will it be ready?
*kâdü tsha-giy ray?* ག་དུས་ཚར་གྱི་རེད།

Do you fix cameras?
*parchay so-chö gyâb-ki yöbay?* པར་ཆས་བཟོ་བཅོས་བརྒྱབ་ཀྱི་ཡོད་པས།

| | | |
|---|---|---|
| camera | *parchay* | པར་ཆས། |
| film | *phing-sho* | ཕིང་ཤོག |
| B&W film | *phing-sho tshön-ta mepa* | ཕིང་ཤོག་ཚོན་མདོག་མེད་པ |
| colour film | *phing-sho tshon-ta chen* | ཕིང་ཤོག་ཚོན་མདོག་ཅན |
| colour slide | *slide phing-sho tshon-ta chen* | ས་ལའིཌ་ཕིང་ཤོག་ཚོན་མདོག་ཅན |
| flash | *parchay-kiy log wö* | པར་ཆས་ཀྱི་གློག |
| lens | *parshay* | པར་ཤེལ། |
| light metre | *wö-tshay gyap-yak* | འོད་ཚད་བརྒྱབ་ཡག |

## Smoking

| | | |
|---|---|---|
| cigarettes | *thama* | ཐ་མག |
| lighter | *may paryak* | མེ་སྤྱར་ཡག |
| matches | *musiy/tsâg-ta* | སུ་སེ/ཚག་ཏ |
| pipe | *tuten-dong* | དུ་འཐེན་མདོང |
| tobacco | *dothâg shib-shib* | མདོ་ཁག་ཞིབ་ཞིབ |

A packet of cigarettes, please.
*thama gâm-chig nâng ro* ཐ་མག་སྒམ་གཅིག་གནང་རོགས།

Do you have a light?
*kayrâng-la may paryak yawbay?* ཁྱེད་རང་ལ་མེ་སྤྱར་ཡག་ཡོད་པས།

Do you mind if I smoke?
*ngay thama ten-nah* ངས་ཐ་མག་འཐེན་ན་འགྲིག་གི་རེད་པས།
*dig-giy rebay?*
Please don't smoke.
*thama ma-tenrog nâng* ཐ་མག་མ་འཐེན་རོགས་གནང་།
I'm trying to give up.
*thama choyak-la tâb-shay* ཐ་མག་གཏོང་ཡག་ལ་ཐབས་ཤེས་བྱེད་ཀྱི་ཡོད།
*chay-kiy yö*

## Weights & Measures

| | | |
|---|---|---|
| gram | *garam* | གྲ་རམ |
| kilogram | *kilogaram/chi-gya* | ཀི་ལོ་གྲ་རམ/སྐྱི་རྒྱ |
| pound | *pon* | པའོན |
| millimetre | *milimiyter* | མི་ལི་མི་ཊར |
| centimetre | *centimiyter* | སེན་གྲི་མི་ཊར |
| metre | *miyter/chiti* | མི་ཊར/སྐྱི་ཏི |
| kilometre | *kilomiyter/chiliy/guli* | ཀི་ལོ་མི་ཊར/སྐྱི་ལི/གུང་ལི |
| half a litre | *liter cheka* | ལི་ཊར་ཕྱེད་ཀ |
| litre | *liter* | ལི་ཊར |

## Sizes & Quantities

| | | |
|---|---|---|
| big | *chempo* | ཆེན་པོ |
| bigger | *chewa* | ཆེ་བ |
| biggest | *cheshö* | ཆེ་ཤོས |
| small | *chung chung* | ཆུང་ཆུང |
| smaller | *chung-nga* | ཆུང་ང |
| smallest | *chung-shö* | ཆུང་ཤོས |
| enough | *dâng-pa* | འདང་ངས་པ |
| few | *kâshay* | ཁ་ཤས |
| heavy | *jibo* | ལྗིད་པོ |
| less | *nyun-wa* | ཉུང་བ |
| light | *yângbo* | ཡང་པོ |
| a little bit | *totsi* | དོག་ཙམ |
| long | *ring-bo* | རིང་པོ |
| many | *mâng-bo* | མང་པོ |
| more | *mâng-wa* | མང་བ |
| much | *shay-tah* | ཞེ་དྲགས |
| short | *thung-thung* | ཐུང་ཐུང |
| some | *kâshay* | ཁ་ཤས |
| tall | *ringbo/thopo* | རིང་པོ/མཐོ་པོ |
| too much/many | *mâng drâgpa* | མང་དྲགས་པ |

## Some Useful Words

| | | |
|---|---|---|
| backpack | *gya-phay* | རྒྱབ་ཁྲ |
| bag | *bag-la/jola* | འབེག་ལག/ཇོལ |
| battery | *logshu-men* | གློག་འཕྲུལ་གྱི་སྨན |

| | | |
|---|---|---|
| bottle | *shaytâm* | ཤེལ་དམ |
| box | *gâm* | སྒྲོམ |
| brass | *râg* | རག |
| button | *tebjü* | ཐེབ་འཇུ |
| candles | *yâng-la* | ཡང་ལ |
| cheap | *kepo* | ཁེ་པོ |
| discount | *gong châgpa* | གོང་བཅག་པ |
| gold | *say* | གསེར |
| handmade | *lâg-sö* | ལག་བཟོས |
| mirror | *shay-go* | ཤེལ་སྒོ |
| needle (sewing) | *(tshen-po  gyâb-ya)* *kâb* | (ཚེམ་པོ་རྒྱབ་ཡག) ཁབ |
| packet | *gâm/dri-thum* | སྒྲོམ/སྒྲིལ་འཐུམས |
| plastic | *pöka* | སྤོས་དཀར |
| receipt | *chung-zin* | བྱུང་འཛིན |

# Health

If you fall ill in Lhasa or in one of the other larger towns, you can be treated by either those who practise Western medicine or by those who practise traditional Tibetan medicine. Western medical treatment is generally obtained at the People's or Chinese hospitals *(mimang menkang* or *gyâmi menkang)* and Tibetan medicine at the *mentisikang* (also called Tibetan hospital – *pöbay menkang).* The People's hospitals have some Tibetan doctors and staff but generally they speak Chinese. The Tibetan hospitals generally use Tibetan.

I am sick.
   *nga nâgiy du*               ང་ན་གི་འདུག

My friend is sick.
   *ngay drogpo nâgiy du*      ངའི་གྲོགས་པོ་ན་གི་འདུག

Get me a doctor at once.
   *âmchi lâm-sâng kay*
   *ton-rog nâng*          ཨེམ་ཆི་ལམ་སང་སྐད་གཏོང་རོགས་གནང་།

Is there a doctor who speaks
English?
   *inji shinken âmchi yaw rebay?*    དབྱིན་ཇི་ཤེས་མཁན་ཨེམ་ཆི་ཡོད་རེད་པས།

Where is the …? ... *kâba du?* ᡱ᠊ᠨᠠᠠᠠ᠊ᠨᠷᠨᠨ

   chemist/pharmacy   *men tshong-khâng*   ᠨᠠᠠᠨ᠊ᠨᠨᠨ

   doctor   *âmchi*   ᠨᠠᠠᠨ

   hospital   *men-khâng*   ᠨᠠᠠᠨᠨ

## Complaints

I've been ill for ... days.
   *nga nânay nyimâ ... chinsong*   ᠨᠨᠨᠨᠨᠨ᠊ᠨᠨᠨ

I feel/am ...   *nga ...-giy du*   ᠨ᠊ᠨᠨᠨ

   nauseous   *kyong-may lâng*   ᠨᠨᠨᠨᠨ

   dizzy   *guyu kaw*   ᠨᠨᠨᠨᠨ

   shivering   *dâr*   ᠨᠨᠨ

I burned my ...   *ngay ... tshig chung*   ᠨᠨ᠊ᠨᠨᠨ᠊ᠨᠨᠨ

   hand   *lagpâ*   ᠨᠨᠨ

   foot   *kangpâ*   ᠨᠨᠨ

I feel feverish.
   *nga tsawâ gyay-sha*   ᠨᠨᠨᠨᠨᠨᠨ

I've been bitten by
something.
   *nga-la chig-giy so gyâb sha*   ᠨᠨᠨᠨᠨᠨᠨᠨᠨᠨ

I'm having trouble breathing.
   *nga ug tong-yak kâgpo du*   ᠨᠨᠨᠨᠨᠨᠨᠨᠨᠨᠨ

I've been vomiting.
   *nga kyug-giy du*   ᠨᠨᠨᠨᠨᠨ

It hurts here.
   *day nâtsa gyâgi du*   ᠨᠨᠨᠨᠨᠨᠨ

I can't sleep.
   *nyi khu-giy mindu*      གཉིད་བཀུགས་གི་མིན་འདུག

| I/She/He has ... | *nga/mo/ko ... giy* | ང་/མོ་/ཁོ་ ----- གིས། |
|---|---|---|
| altitude sickness | *lâdu na* | ལ་དུག་ན |
| anaemia | *trâg nyâm-pay na-tsha na* | ཁྲག་ཉམས་པའི་ན་ཚ |
| asthma | *ug-tshâng lonay na* | དབུགས་འཚང་ལོ་ན་ན |
| a blister | *chugân na* | ཆུ་སྒར་ན |
| a boil | *nyem-bu na* | གཉིན་འབུར་ན |
| conjunctivitis | *mig-nay na* | མིག་ནད་ན |
| a cold/flu | *châmba na* | ཆམ་པ་ན |
| a cough | *lo-gyâb* | ལོ་བརྒྱབ |
| dehydration | *shâlon thenpay na-tsha na* | ཤ་རྣོན་འཐེན་པའི་ནཚ་ན |
| diabetes | *chemakâray na-tsha na* | བྱེ་མ་ཀ་རའི་ན་ཚ་ན |
| dysentery | *dro-gaw shepay na-tsha disentriy na* | གྲོད་ཁོག་བཤལ་པའི་ན་ཚ་ནི་རི་ན |
| a fever | *tsha-wa na* | ཚ་བ་ན |
| frostbite | *khyâg-bö* | བཁྱགས་བྲོས |
| glandular fever | *trenay tsha-wa na* | སྐྲན་ནད་ཚ་བ་ན |
| headache | *gaw na* | མགོ་ན |
| hepatitis | *chin-nay na* | མཆིན་ནད་ན |
| an itch | *sab-ra lang* | ཟ་ར་ལང |
| malaria | *malariya na* | མ་ལེ་རི་ཡ་ན |

| | | |
|---|---|---|
| a migraine | *yama natsha maygrayn na* | ཡ་མ་ནཚ་ཤིགས་ན |
| rheumatism | *ru-tshig na* | རུས་ཚིགས་ན |
| a stomachache | *dro-kok na* | གྲོད་ཁོག་ན |
| sunstroke | *tsha-du na* | ཚ་དུག་ན |
| a toothache | *so na* | སོ་ན |
| typhoid | *tshanay-tayfoyd na* | ཚ་ནད་ཐྱོཕོཌ་ན |
| venereal disease | *drangshi rig-giy natshâ chig* | གྲང་གཞིའི་རིགས་ཀྱི་ནཚ་ཆིག་ |

I am constipated.
  *nga châb-chen bâb-kiy mindu* ངར་ཆབ་ཆེན་འབབ་ཀྱི་མི་འདུག

I have a cramp (in calf).
  *nya gyur sha* ངའི་རྒྱུ་འགྱུར་ཤག

I have a cut.
  *nga-la ma sö-song* ང་ལ་མ་བཟོས་སོང་

I have diarrhoea.
  *nga dro-kok shay-giy* ང་གྲོད་ཁོག་བཤལ་གྱིས

I have food poisoning.
  *nga-la say-dhug phog-sha* ང་ལ་ཟས་དུག་ཕོག་ཤག

I have indigestion.
  *nga toh jugiy mindu* ང་ཏོ་འཇུ་གྱི་མི་འདུག

I have an infection.
  *nga-la gönay-chig gö sha* ང་ལ་འགོས་ནད་ཅིག་འགོས་ཤག

I have lice.
  *nga-la shig gö sha* ང་ལ་ཤིག་འགོས་ཤག

I have low/high blood pressure.
  *ngay tâg-shay thopo/mâpo ray* ངའི་ཁྲག་ཤེད་དམའ་པོ/མཐོ་པོ་རེད

I have a rash.
  *nga-la thor-drum gö sha* ང་ལ་ཐོར་འབུམ་འགོས་ཤག

I have a sore throat.
*n: ngay migpa nâng-la ma châg-sha*  ངའི་མིད་པ་ནང་ལ་མ་ཆགས་ཤག

I have sunburn.
*nga nyib-tâg thep song*  ང་ཉི་བཀག་འཐེབས་སོང་།

My foot is swollen.
*ngay kânpa trângsha*  ངའི་ཀང་པ་སྦོས་ཤག

I have a temperature.
*nga tsha-tshay gyay-sha*  ང་ཚ་ཚད་རྒྱས་ཤག

I have worms.
*ngay khog-pay nang bu du*  ངའི་ཁོག་པའི་ནང་བུ་འདུག

## Women's Health

I'd like to see a female doctor.
*nga kyeman âmchi-chig tendö yö*  ང་སྐྱེ་དམན་ཨེམ་ཆི་ཞིག་བལྟེན་འདོད་ཡོད།

I want to see a gynaecologist.
*nga mo-tshen menchay khaypa chig tendö yö*  ང་མོ་མཚན་སྨན་དཔྱད་མཁས་པ་གཅིག་བལྟེན་འདོད་ཡོད།

I'm on the pill.
*nga kyegaw gâkyak men sagiy yo*  ང་སྐྱེ་སྒོ་བཀག་འགལ་གྱི་སྨན་ཟ་གི་ཡོད།

I'm pregnant.
*nga-la pugu kay-yak yo*  ང་ལ་ཕྲུ་གུ་སྐྱེ་ཡག་ཡོད།

I haven't had my period for ... months.
*nga-la da-tshen mabâb-nay dawa ... chinsong*  ང་ལ་ཟླ་མཚན་མ་བབས་ནས་ཟླ་བ ..... ཕྱིན་སོང་།

maternity hospital
*pugu kay-say menkhâng*  ཕྲུ་གུ་སྐྱེ་སའི་སྨན་ཁང་

## Allergies

| I'm allergic to ... | ... nga-la tö-giy may | –ང་ལ་སྟོད་གྱི་གི་མེད། |
| antibiotics | gonay ngonkog-kiy men rig | བགོས་ནད་སྔོན་འགོག་གི་སྨན་རིགས། |
| penicillin | gonay kâgyak men peniysilin | ནད་འབུ་བཀག་འགག་གི་སྨན་པན་ནི་སི་ལིན། |

## Parts of the Body

My ... is sprained/broken.
  ngay ... chusha/châsha    ངའི་ ... འཁྱུད་ཤ་ཤག/ ཆག་ཤག

I can't move my ...
  ngay ... gul-kyog thupki mindu    ངའི་ ... སྐུལ་སྐྱོག་ཐུབ་ཀྱི་མིན་འདུག

| My ... hurts. | ngay ... nâgiy | ངའི་ ... ན་གི་ས། |
| appendix | gyuma | རྒྱུ་མ། |
| back | gyâb | རྒྱབ། |
| chest | pâng-gaw | བྲང་ཁོག |
| chin | melay/ogma | མ་མལ་ལི/ཝོག་མ། |
| face | dong | གདོང་། |
| heart | nying | སྙིང་། |
| hip | chigo | དཔྱི་མགོ། |
| knee | pui-mo | པུས་མོ། |
| leg | kângpâ | རྐང་པ། |
| mouth | kha | ཁ། |
| nose | nâ-kug | སྣ་ཁུག |
| skin . | sha pâg-pa | ཤ་པགས་པ། |
| spine | gaytshig | སྒལ་ཚིགས། |
| stomach | drokok | གྲོད་ཁོག |

head
*gaw*
མགོ

eye
*mig*
མིག

ear
*âmjo*
ཨམ་ཆོ

shoulder
*pungpa/trâgpa*
དཔུང་པ/ཕྲག་པ

neck
*kay*
སྐེ

arm
*lagpâ*
ལག་ངར

elbow
*drumo*
གྲུ་མོ

hand
*lâgpâ*
ལག་པ

finger
*dzugu*
མཛུབ་གུ

foot
*kângpa*
རྐང་པ

ankle
*kâng-tshig*
རྐང་ཚིགས

| teeth | *so* | སོ |
| throat | *migpa* | མིད་པ |
| tongue | *chay* | ལྕེ |
| tonsils | *chaytsa yeyon tendog* | ལྕེ་རྩ་གཡས་གཡོན་སྐྲན་རྡོག |

## *At the Chemist*

I need something for …
   *… chaydu chig go*    ཚེད་དུ་གཅིག་དགོས།

Do I need a prescription
for …
   *… nyowa-la âmchiy men-zin*    ཉོ་བ་ལ་ཨེམ་ཆིའི་སྨན་བཙིན་དགོས་ཀྱི་རེད་པས།
   *gawgiy rebay?*

How many should I take a day?
   *nyima reray ten kâtsay sa*    ཉི་མ་རེ་རེ་ལ་བཏེན་ཀ་ཚད་ཟ་དགོས་རེད།
   *gawray?*

| | | |
|---|---|---|
| antibiotics | *gonay ngonkog-kiy men* | འགོས་ནད་སྔོན་འགོག་སྨན། |
| antidiarrhoeal drug | *throgaw shay-gyu kâya-kiy men* | གྲོད་ཁོག་བཤལ་རྒྱུ་བཀག་པ་ལ་གི་སྨན། |
| antiseptic | *naybhu kâyak men* | ནད་འབུ་བཀག་པ་ལ་སྨན། |
| aspirin | *esbirin/gawmen* | ཨེ་སི་པི་རིན/ མགོ་སྨན། |
| bandage (gauze) | *mati/menray* | མ་དཀྲི/ སྨན་རས། |
| Band-aid (plaster) | *koyö* | སོ་ཡོལ། |
| medicine for blood pressure | *trâg-shay châya-giy men* | ཁྲག་ཤེད་གཅའ་བ་ལ་སྨན། |
| cold/flu medicine | *châmbay-men* | ཆམ་པའི་སྨན། |
| contraceptives | *kyegaw kâyâk-kiy men* | སྐྱེ་སྒོ་བཀག་པ་ལ་སྨན། |
| cough medicine | *lo-men* | གློ་སྨན། |
| eye medicine | *mig-men* | མིག་སྨན། |
| iodine | *go-nay kâyak iodine* | འགོས་ནད་བཀག་པ་ལ་ཨ་ཨོ་དིན། |
| medicine for fever | *tsha-way men* | ཚ་བའི་སྨན། |
| medicine for headaches | *gaw-men* | མགོ་སྨན། |

| | | |
|---|---|---|
| laxatives | *châpchen bâyâkiy men* | ཚབ་ཆེན་བབ་འགྱག་གི་སྨན་ |
| pain killer | *natshâ chaya-kiy men* | ནཚགཐལ་འལ་གི་སྨན་ |
| throat medicine | *migbay men* | མིད་པའི་སྨན་ |
| vitamins | *topgyay men* | སྟོབས་བསྐྱེད་སྨན་ |
| worm medicine | *bumen* | འབུ་སྨན་ |

## *At the Dentist*

Is there a good dentist here?
*dipar so-âmchi yâgpo chig*    འདི་པར་སོ་ཨེམ་ཆི་ཡག་པོ་གཅིག་ཡོད་རེད་པས།
*yaw rebay?*

I have a toothache.
*nga so nâgiy*    ང་སོ་ན་གིས།

I don't want it extracted.
*nga so tön-dö may*    ང་སོ་འདོན་འདོད་མེད།

Please give me an anaesthetic.
*nga-la birmen nang rog*    ང་ལ་སྦྱིར་སྨན་གནང་རོགས།

## You Might Hear

Where does it hurt?
*na-tsha kaba dâng-giy du?*    ནཚ་ག་པར་གཏོང་གི་འདུག

How long have you been ill?
*kayrang nanay, nyimâ kâtsay*    ཁྱེད་རང་ན་ནས་ཉིན་མ་ཚད་ཚོན་སོང་།
*chinsong?*

| | | |
|---|---|---|
| I'll take your ... | *ngay kayrâng-kiy ...* *dâgiy-yin* | ངས་ཁྱེད་རང་གི་ ⸺ ལུ་གི་ཨིན། |
| blood | *tra* | ཁྲག |
| blood pressure | *trâg-shay chechung* | ཁྲག་ཤེད་ཆེ་ཆུང་ |
| pulse | *tsa* | རྩ་ |

| | | |
|---|---|---|
| stool (sample) | *châpchen* | ཆབ་ཆེན། |
| temperature | *tsha-wâ* | ཚ་བ། |
| urine (sample) | *chinpâ/châpsang* | གཅིན་པ/ཆབ་སང་ |

Open your mouth.
  *kha dong-dâ*  ཁ་གདོངས་དང་།

Take a deep breath.
  *ug shug-chay ya ten-dâ*  དབུགས་ཤུགས་ཆེ་ཡར་ཐེན་དང་།

Please cough.
  *lo gyöndâ*  གློ་བརྒྱུན་དང་།

I'll give you an injection.
  *ngay kâp gyâgiy-yin*  ངས་ཁབ་བརྒྱབ་ཀྱི་ཡིན།

I'll give you medicine.
  *ngay men daygiy-yin*  ངས་སྨན་སྤྲད་ཀྱི་ཡིན།

| Take this ... a day. | *diy nyimâ rayray ...* | འདི་ནི་ཉི་མ་རེ་རེ་ལ་ ...... |
| | *chöronâng* | མཆོད་རོགས་གནང་། |
| twice | *teng nyiy-ray* | ཐེང་གཉིས་རེ། |
| three times | *teng soom-ray* | ཐེང་གསུམ་རེ། |
| four times | *teng shiy-ray* | ཐེང་བཞི་རེ། |

| Take ... pill(s) each | *teng rayray riybu ...* | ཐེང་རེ་རེ་ལ་རིལ་བུ་ ...... |
| time. | *sagaw ray* | བཟའ་དགོས་རེད། |
| one | *reray* | རེ་རེ། |
| two | *nyiy-ray* | གཉིས་རེ། |
| three | *sum-ray* | གསུམ་རེ། |

Your illness is not serious.
  *kayrâng-kiy natsha dugja mindu*  ཁྱེད་རང་གི་ན་ཚ་སྡུག་ཆགས་ཆགས་མིན་འདུག

## Some Useful Words & Phrases

I have a heart condition.
  *nga-la nying-giy na-tsha yö*  ང་ལ་སྙིང་གི་ན་ཚ་ཡོད།

I am diabetic.
  *nga-la chemakâray na-tsha yö*  ང་ལ་བྱེ་མ་ཀ་རའི་ན་ཚ་ཡོད།

I am epileptic.
  *nga-la sa-drip yo*  ང་ལ་ཟའ་གྲིབ་ཡོད།

I have been vaccinated.
  *nga na-tsha ngon-gokiy*
  *menkâb gya-tsa yin*  ང་ན་ཚ་སྔོན་འགོག་གི་སྨན་ཁབ་བརྒྱབ་ཚར་ཡིན།

I have my own syringe.
  *menkâb ngarâng la yö*  སྨན་ཁབ་ང་རང་ལ་ཡོད།

| | | |
|---|---|---|
| accident | *dongthup gyâbpa* | གདོང་ཐུག་བརྒྱབ་པ། |
| acupuncture | *tsakâb gyab-pa* | ཚ་ཁབ་བརྒྱབ་པ། |
| addiction | *kya-lâng shorwa* | སྐྱག་ལང་ཤོར་བ། |
| bite (insect) | *bhu so gyâbpa* | འབུ་སོ་བརྒྱབ་པ། |
| bite (dog) | *khi so gyâbpa* | ཁྱི་སོ་བརྒྱབ་པ། |
| bleeding | *trâg dzâgpa* | ཁྲག་འཛག་པ། |
| blood pressure | *trâg-shay* | ཁྲག་ཤེད། |
| blood test | *trâg tâg-jay* | ཁྲག་བརྟག་དཔྱད། |
| body | *sug-po* | གཟུགས་པོ། |
| bone | *rugu* | རུས་ཀོག |
| condom | *ligshoop* | ལྡིག་ཤུབས། |
| contraceptives | *kyegok kâya* | སྐྱེ་འགོག་བཀག་ཐབས། |
| faeces | *châpchen/kyâgpa* | ཆབ་ཆེན/སྐྱག་པ། |
| injection | *kâb gyâb-pa* | ཁབ་བརྒྱབ་པ། |
| injury | *may-kyön* | རྨས་སྐྱོན། |

| | | |
|---|---|---|
| medicine | *men* | སྨན |
| menstruation | *da-tshen/da-trög* | ཟླ་མཚན/ཟླ་ཁྲག |
| nausea | *kyug-may lângwa/*<br>*shenlog gyâpa* | སྐྱུག་མེར་ལང་བ/ཞེན་ལོག་བརྒྱབ་པ |
| ointment | *ma-men* | རྨ་སྨན |
| operation | *shâgjö* | གཤགས་བཅོས |
| oxygen | *sogzin lung* | སོག་འཛིན་རླུང |
| pus | *nâg* | རྣག |
| urine | *chinpâ/châpsang* | གཅིན་པ/ཆབ་སང |
| vitamins | *topgyay men* | སྟོབས་བསྐྱེད་སྨན |
| wound | *ma* | རྨ |

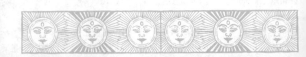

# Time, Dates & Festivals

Time your visit to coincide with one of the major festivals and your experience of this country will be even richer. For key festivals, turn to page 136.

## *Telling the Time*

To state the time, refer to Numbers & Amounts, page 140, and just add the suffix *-bâ* to the number you want.

What time is it?
    *tanda chutsö kâtsö-ray?*     ད་སྒྲ་ཆོད་ག་ཆོད་རེད།

(Now) it's ...     *(tânda) chutsö ... ray*   (དང་)ཆོད་ ... རེད།
  o'clock

  two             *nyibâ*              གཉིས་པ
  five             *ngabâ*            ལྔ་པ

There are some unusual ones, however, which must be learnt separately:

(Now) It's one o'clock.
    *(tanda) chutsö tâng-po ray*   (དང་)ཆུ་ཆོད་དང་པོ་རེད།
(Now) It's midnight.
    *(tanda) gong-da chutsö chunyi ray*   (དང་)དགོང་དག་ཆུ་ཆོད་བཅུ་གཉིས་རེད།

TIME, DATES & FESTIVALS

(Now) It's noon.
    *(tanda) nyi-gung chutsö*      (དང་)ཉིན་གུང་ཆུ་ཚོད་བཅུ་གཉིས་རེད།
    *chunyi ray*

The term for 'half past' is *chekâ*, and for 'quarter past' is *karma chöngâ*:

It's two thirty.
    *tânda chutsö nyi dâng chekâ*      ད་ལྟ་ཆུ་ཚོད་གཉིས་དང་ཕྱེད་ཀ་རེད།
    *ray*
It's quarter past six.
    *tandâ chutsö trug dâng karma*      ད་ལྟ་ཆུ་ཚོད་དྲུག་དང་སྐར་མ་བཅོ་ལྔ་རེད།
    *chöngâ ray*

## Some Useful Phrases

I'll come in ...      *nga karma ... nâng*      ང་སྐར་མ་ ...... ནང་ཡོང་གི་ཡིན།
minutes.      *yong-giy yin*

    10      *chu*      བཅུ

    45      *shi-chu shay-ngâ*      བཞི་བཅུ་ཞེ་ལྔ

I'll come in ... hours.
    *nga chutsö ... nâng yong-giy yin*      ང་ཆུ་ཚོད་ ...... ནང་ཡོང་གི་ཡིན།
What time is dinner?
    *gongda kala chutsö kâtsö-la*      དགོང་དག་ཁ་ལག་ཆུ་ཚོད་ག་ཚོད་ལ་རེད།
    *ray?*
Please bring the food in
10 minutes.
    *karma chu-nâng kala kay*      སྐར་མ་བཅུའི་ནང་ཁ་ལག་འཁྱེར་ཡོང་རོགས་གནང
    *yong-ronâng*

## Days

Monday      *sa dawa*      གཟའ་ཟླ་བ
Tuesday      *sa migma*      གཟའ་མིག་དམར

| Wednesday | *sa lhagbâ* | གཟའ་ལྷག་པ་ |
| Thursday | *sa phubu* | གཟའ་ཕུར་བུ་ |
| Friday | *sa pasang* | གཟའ་པ་སངས་ |
| Saturday | *sa pembâ* | གཟའ་སྤེན་པ་ |
| Sunday | *sa nyimâ* | གཟའ་ཉི་མ་ |

## Months

Two calendars are used in Tibet: the traditional lunar-based system where each month has 30 days, and the Gregorian calendar as used in the West. The lunar New Year generally occurs about six weeks after the Western New Year, which means that the first month in the Tibetan calendar usually begins in mid-February. In both calendars, however, there are 12 months which are simply referred to as the '1st month', the '2nd month', etc.

| 1st month | *dawa tâng-po* | ཟླ་བ་དང་པོ་ |
| 2nd month | *dawa nyiy-bâ* | ཟླ་བ་གཉིས་པ་ |
| 3rd month | *dawa sumba* | ཟླ་བ་གསུམ་པ་ |
| 4th month | *dawa shibâ* | ཟླ་བ་བཞི་པ་ |
| 5th month | *dawa ngaba* | ཟླ་བ་ལྔ་པ་ |
| 6th month | *dawa trugbâ* | ཟླ་བ་དྲུག་པ་ |
| 7th month | *dawa dünbâ* | ཟླ་བ་བདུན་པ་ |
| 8th month | *dawa gyaybâ* | ཟླ་བ་བརྒྱད་པ་ |
| 9th month | *dawa gubâ* | ཟླ་བ་དགུ་པ་ |
| 10th month | *dawa chubâ* | ཟླ་བ་བཅུ་པ་ |
| 11th month | *dawa chu-chigbâ* | ཟླ་བ་བཅུ་གཅིག་པ་ |
| 12th month | *dawa chu-nyibâ* | ཟླ་བ་བཅུ་གཉིས་པ་ |

If more precision is required, you can substitute *chinda* (Western month) or *pöndâ* (Tibetan month) for *dawa* which just means 'month'. Thus February may be *chinda nyiy-bâ*, or *pöndâ tang-po* depending on the calendar being used.

## Dates

What date is it today?
(Western calendar)

| | |
|---|---|
| *tering chi-tshay kâtsö ray?* | དེ་རིང་ཕྱི་ཚེས་ག་ཚོད་རེད། |

It's 28 June.

| | |
|---|---|
| *tering chinda trugbay tshay nyishu tsab-gyay ray* | དེ་རིང་ཕྱི་ཟླ་དྲུག་པའི་ཚེས་ཉི་ཤུ་རྩ་བརྒྱད་རེད། |

It's 3 June.

| | |
|---|---|
| *tering chinda trugbay tshay soom ray* | དེ་རིང་ཕྱི་ཟླ་དྲུག་པའི་ཚེས་གསུམ་རེད། |

It's 1 April.

| | |
|---|---|
| *tering chinda shibay tshay chig ray* | དེ་རིང་ཕྱི་ཟླ་བཞི་པའི་ཚེས་གཅིག་རེད། |

## During the Day

| | | |
|---|---|---|
| sunrise | *nyin-ma shardu* | ཉིན་མ་ཤར་དུས |
| morning | *shawgay* | ཞོགས་ཀས་ |
| noon | *nyin-gung* | ཉིན་གུང་ |
| afternoon | *chito* | ཕྱི་དྲོ |
| evening | *gongda* | དགོང་དག |
| sundown | *nyi-noob* | ཉི་ནུབ |
| midnight | *nâm-chay* | ནམ་ཕྱེ |

## Time
### Present

| | | |
|---|---|---|
| today | *dering* | དེ་རིང་ |
| this morning | *târâng shawgay* | དེ་རིང་ཞོགས་ཀས་ |
| this evening | *togong* | དོ་གོང་ |
| this week | *sakhaw diy/dun-tâg diy* | གཟའ་འཁོར་འདི་/བདུན་ཕྲག་འདི་ |
| this month | *dawa diy* | ཟླ་བ་འདི་ |
| this year | *tâlo/lo diy* | ད་ལོ་/ལོ་འདི་ |
| immediately | *dânta-râng* | ད་ལྟ་རང་ |
| now | *dânda* | ད་ལྟ་ |

### Past

| | | |
|---|---|---|
| yesterday | *kaysâ* | ཁ་ས་ |
| day before yesterday | *kay nyin-mo* | ཁེ་ཉིན་མོ་ |
| yesterday morning | *kaysa shawgay* | ཁ་ས་ཞོགས་ཀས་ |
| yesterday evening | *dâng-gong* | མདང་དགོང་ |
| last week | *sâkhaw ngön-ma/ dunta ngön-ma* | གཟའ་འཁོར་སྔོན་མ་/ བདུན་ཕྲག་སྔོན་མ་ |
| last month | *dawa ngön-ma* | ཟླ་བ་སྔོན་མ་ |
| last year | *dânyi/lo ngön-ma* | ན་ནིང་/ལོ་སྔོན་མ་ |

### Future

| | | |
|---|---|---|
| tomorrow | *sâ-nyin* | སང་ཉིན་ |
| tomorrow morning | *sâng-shaw* | སང་ཞོག་ |
| tomorrow evening | *sâng-nyi gongda/ sâng-gong* | སང་ཉི་དགོང་དག/ སང་དགོང་ |

| next week | sakhaw jaymâ/ dun-tâg jaymâ | གཟའ་འཁོར་རྗེས་མ/ བདུན་ཕྲག་རྗེས་མ |
| next month | dawa jaymâ | ཟླ་བ་རྗེས་མ |
| next year | lo juma/tüsang | ལོ་རྗེས་མ/དུས་སང |

## Seasons

| spring | chi-ka | དཔྱིད་ཀ |
| summer | yar-kha | དབྱར་ཁ |
| autumn | tön-kha | སྟོན་ཁ |
| winter | gön-kha | དགུན་ཁ |

## Religious & National Festivals

Anyone who is lucky enough to attend a Tibetan festival should have the opportunity to see performances of *cham,* a ritual, masked dance performed by monks and lamas.

### New Year Festival (losar)  ལོ་གསར

The 1st day of the first Tibetan month. Lhasa is at its most colourful during this festival. Pilgrims make incense offerings, and everyone dresses in their finest. Performances of Tibetan drama may also be seen.

**Great Prayer Festival (monlâm chenmo)** སྨོན་ལམ་ཆེན་མོ
Held midway through the 1st Tibetan months.

*saga dawa* ས་ག་ཟླ་བ
The anniversary of Buddha's birth, death and enlightenment, and is celebrated on the 15th day of the 4th Tibetan month. It is an occasion for outdoor operas.

**Incence Burning Festival (dzâmling chisâng)** འཛམ་གླིང་སྤྱི་བསང
Occurs on the 15th day of the 5th Tibetan month.

**Lhasa Shoton Festival (lhasa shoton)** ལྷ་ས་ཞོ་སྟོན
Held on the 2nd day of the 7th Tibetan month. This is a Yoghurt festival during which operas and masked dances are held, and locals enjoy picnics.

**Lhasa Farmer Festival (lhasa ong-kor)** ལྷ་ས་འོང་བསྐོར
Often occurs during the 7th Tibetan month.

*trung-kar dü-chen* འཁྲུངས་སྐར་དུས་ཆེན
His Holiness the Dalai Lama's birthday. It is celebrated on the 6th day of the 7th Western month (July).

### chokor du-chen
ཆོས་འཁོར་དུས་ཆེན

The remembrance of Buddha's first discourse. It takes place on the 4th day of the 6th Tibetan month.

### lha-bâb dü-chen
ལྷ་བབས་དུས་ཆེན

The remembrance of Buddha's descent from heaven in a celebration on the 22nd day of the 9th Tibetan month. Many pilgrims go to Lhasa for this occasion.

### ganden ngâm-chö
དགའ་ལྡན་ལྔ་མཆོད

Also known as the Tsong Khapa anniversary, it is on the 25th day of the 10th Tibetan month.

### gu-thok
དགུ་གཏོར

A festival to banish evil spirits. It is held on the 29th day of the 12th Tibetan month.

## Some Useful Words

| | | |
|---|---|---|
| a while ago | yün-tsâm ngön-la | ཡུན་ཚམ་སྔོན་ལ |
| after | jayla | རྗེས་ལ |
| always | tâgpa/chârchen | རྟག་པར/འཆར་ཅན |
| before | ngön-la | སྔོན་ལ |
| century | gyatâg | བརྒྱ་ཕྲག་གཅིག |
| day | nyin-ma | ཉིན་མ |
| early | nga-po | སྔ་པོ |
| every day | nyin-tar | ཉིན་ལྟར |
| forever | tâgtu | རྟག་ཏུ |
| fortnight | sakor nyiy | བདུན་ཕྲག་གཉིས |
| late | chipo | ཕྱི་པོ |

TIME, DATES & FESTIVALS

| long ago | *ngamo ngamo* | སྔ་མོ་སྔ་མོ་ |
| month | *dawa* | ཟླ་བ་ |
| never | *nâm-yang* | ནམ་ཡང་ |
| night | *gongda/tshen-mo* | དགོང་དག/མཚན་མོ་ |
| not any more | *yâng-kyamin/ chinchay-min* | ཡང་སྐྱར་མིན/ཕྱིན་ཆད་མིན་ |
| not yet | *tânda yâng may* | ད་ལྟ་ཡང་མེད་ |
| recently | *nye-jah* | ཉེ་ཆར་ |
| sometimes | *tshâm tshâm-la* | མཚམས་མཚམས་ |
| soon | *gyog-po* | མགྱོགས་པོ་ |
| these days | *teng-sâng* | དེང་སང་ |
| week | *sakhaw/dün-tâg* | བདུན་ཕྲག/གཟའ་འཁོར་ |
| year | *lo* | ལོ་ |
| ... years ago | *lo ... ngân-la* | ལོ་......སྔོན་ལ་ |

# Numbers & Amounts

Learn the numbers one to nine, and it will help you see the patterns in the higher numbers. Happy counting!

## Cardinal Numbers

| 0  | *laykor*    | གྲངས་གོང་ |
|----|-------------|------------|
| 1  | *chig*      | གཅིག་ |
| 2  | *nyi*       | གཉིས་ |
| 3  | *sum*       | གསུམ་ |
| 4  | *shi*       | བཞི་ |
| 5  | *nga*       | ལྔ་ |
| 6  | *trug*      | དྲུག་ |
| 7  | *dün*       | བདུན་ |
| 8  | *gyay*      | བརྒྱད་ |
| 9  | *gu*        | དགུ་ |
| 10 | *chu*       | བཅུ་ |
| 11 | *chug-chig* | བཅུ་གཅིག་ |
| 12 | *chu-nyi*   | བཅུ་གཉིས་ |
| 13 | *chog-sum*  | བཅུ་གསུམ་ |

| | | |
|---|---|---|
| 14 | *chup-shi* | བཅུ་བཞི། |
| 15 | *chö-nga* | བཅོ་ལྔ། |
| 16 | *chu-trug* | བཅུ་དྲུག |
| 17 | *choop-dün* | བཅུ་བདུན། |
| 18 | *chop-gyay* | བཅོ་བརྒྱད། |
| 19 | *chu-gu* | བཅུ་དགུ། |
| 20 | *nyi-shu/shi shu thâmpa* | ཉི་ཤུ། ཉི་ཤུ་ཕྲག་གཅིག |
| 21 | *nyi-shu tsa-chig* | ཉི་ཤུ་རྩ་གཅིག |
| 22 | *nyi-shu tsa-nyi* | ཉི་ཤུ་རྩ་གཉིས། |
| 30 | *sumchu/sumchu thâmpa* | སུམ་བཅུ། སུམ་བཅུ་ཐམ་པ། |
| 40 | *ship-chu/ship-chu thâmpa* | བཞི་བཅུ། བཞི་བཅུ་ཐམ་པ། |
| 50 | *ngâp-chu/ngâp-chu thâmpa* | ལྔ་བཅུ། ལྔ་བཅུ་ཐམ་པ། |
| 60 | *trug-chu/trug-chu thâmpa* | དྲུག་བཅུ། དྲུག་བཅུ་ཐམ་པ། |
| 70 | *dün-chu/dün-chu thâmpa* | བདུན་བཅུ། བདུན་བཅུ་ཐམ་པ། |
| 80 | *gyây-chu/gyây-chu thâmpa* | བརྒྱད་བཅུ། བརྒྱད་བཅུ་ཐམ་པ། |
| 90 | *gup-chu/gup-chu thâmpa* | དགུ་བཅུ། དགུ་བཅུ་ཐམ་པ། |
| 100 | *gya/gya thâmpa* | བརྒྱ། བརྒྱ་ཐམ་པ། |
| 200 | *nyi-gya* | ཉིས་བརྒྱ། ཉིས་བརྒྱ་ཐམ་པ། |
| 1000 | *chig-dong/dong-ta chig* | ཆིག་སྟོང་། སྟོང་ཕྲག་གཅིག |

| | | |
|---|---|---|
| 2000 | *nyi dong/dong-dra nyi* | ཉིས་སྟོང་/སྟོང་ཕྲག་གཉིས |
| 10,000 | *chig tri/dong-ta chu* | ཁྲི་གཇིག་/སྟོང་ཕྲག་བཅུ |
| 100,000 | *chig-bum/tri chu* | ཁྲི་འབུམ/ཁྲི་བཅུ |
| one million | *saya-chig/bum chu* | ས་ཡ་གཅིག/འབུམ་བཅུ |

## Ordinal Numbers

| | | |
|---|---|---|
| 1st | *tâng-po* | དང་པོ |
| 2nd | *nyiy-bâ* | གཉིས་པ |
| 3rd | *sum-bâ* | གསུམ་པ |
| 4th | *shiy-bâ* | བཞི་པ |
| 5th | *nga-bâ* | ལྔ་པ |
| 6th | *trug-bâ* | དྲུག་པ |
| 7th | *dün-bâ* | བདུན་པ |
| 8th | *gyay-bâ* | བརྒྱད་པ |
| 9th | *gu-bâ* | དགུ་པ |
| 10th | *chu-bâ* | བཅུ་པ |
| 11th | *choogji-bâ* | བཅུ་གཅིག་པ |

## Fractions

| | | |
|---|---|---|
| ¼ | *shiy-jâ chig* | བཞི་ཆ་གཅིག |
| ⅓ | *sum-jâ chig* | གསུམ་ཆ་གཅིག |
| ½ | *chekâ* | ཕྱེད་ཀ |
| ¾ | *shiy-jâ sum* | བཞི་ཆ་གསུམ |
| ⅔ | *sumjâ nyiy* | གསུམ་ཆ་གཉིས |

## Some Useful Words

| | | |
|---|---|---|
| How many? | *kâtsay?* | ག་ཚོད་ |
| a little | *nyung-nyung* | ཉུང་ཉུང་ |
| count (v) | *drâng-ga gyâb* | གྲངས་ཀ་བརྒྱབ་ |
| double | *nyi-dzâg* | ཉི་ཚེག་ |
| dozen | *dhar-tsen chig* | དར་ཚོན་གཅིག་ |
| enough | *dig-song* | འགྲིགས་སོང་ |
| not enough | *dig-mâsong* | འགྲིགས་མ་སོང་ |
| few | *ka-shay/te-tsi* | ཁ་ཤས/དེག་ཙམ་ |
| less | *nyung-wa* | ཉུང་བ་ |
| a lot | *mâng-po* | མང་པོ་ |
| many | *mâng-po* | མང་པོ་ |
| more | *mâng-wa* | མང་བ་ |
| once | *teng-chig* | ཐེངས་གཅིག་ |
| pair | *cha* | ཆ་ |
| percent | *gya-ja* | བརྒྱ་ཆ་ |
| some | *ka-shay* | ཁ་ཤས་ |
| too much | *mâng-trâgsha* | མང་དྲགས་ཁགས་ |
| twice | *teng-nyiy* | ཐེངས་གཉིས་ |

# Vocabulary

## A

| able (to be) | thup-pa/nüpa | ཐུབ་པ/ནུས་པ |
| above | gâng-la | སྒང་ལ |
| abroad | chi-gyal | ཕྱི་རྒྱལ་བ |
| accept (v) | ngo-lan | ངོས་ལེན |
|   I accept. (acknowledge) | ngay ngo-len yö | ངས་ངོས་ལེན་ཡོད། |
|   You accept. | kayrâng-giy ngo-lan du | ཁྱེད་རང་གིས་ངོས་ལེན་འདུག |
| accident | dhon-toop gyâb | གདོན་ཐོགས་བརྒྱབ |
| accommodation | dhö-nay | སྡོད་གནས |
| across | tay-la | བརྒྱད་ལ |
| adaptor | lo-shoog choyak | གློག་ཤུགས་བཅོས་ལག |
| addict | kya-lâng shor | རྐྱ་ལང་ཤོར |
| addiction | kya-lâng showa | རྐྱ་ལང་ཤོར་བ |
| address | kajang | ཁ་བྱང |
| administration | zin-kyong | འཛིན་སྐྱོང |
| admire | tö-pa | བསྟོད་པ |
| admission | nâng zhu | ནང་ཞུགས |
| adventure | yâyu | ཨ་ཡུད |
| advice | lâbja | བསླབ་བྱ |
| advise | lâbja gyâb | བསླབ་བྱ་བརྒྱབ |
| afraid | trâg-pa | སྐྲག་པ |

144

| | | |
|---|---|---|
| after | *jela* | རྗེས་ལ |
| afternoon | *chito* | ཕྱི་དྲོ |
| again | *yâng-kya* | ཡང་སྐྱར |
| against | *khâb-tedu* | ཁ་ཐད་དུ |
| age | *lo* | ལོ |
| agree | *mothün* | མོས་མཐུན |
| I agree. | *ngay mothün yö* | ངས་མོས་མཐུན་ཡོད། |
| You agree. | *kayrâng mothün du* | ཁྱེད་རང་གིས་མོས་མཐུན་འདུག། |
| agriculture | *shing-lay* | ཞིང་ལས |
| ahead | *dünla* | མདུན་དུ |
| aid | *rog chepa* | རོགས་བྱེད་པ |
| AIDS | *aids nay-rig* | ཨེཊས་ནད་རིགས |
| air-conditioned | *drâng-log* | གྲང་གློག |
| airline | *khâlam* | མཁའ་ལམ |
| airmail | *nâmdâg* | གནམ་སྦྲགས |
| alarm clock | *lâng-da tonya chu-tsö* | ལང་བརྡ་གཏོང་ཡས་ཆུད་ཚོད |
| all | *tshâng-ma* | ཚང་མ |
| allow | *chay-chogpa* | བྱེད་ཆོག་པ |
| almost | *phe-chay* | ཕལ་ཆེར |
| alone | *chigpo* | གཅིག་པུ |
| also | *yâng* | ཡང |
| alternative | *remo chenay* | རེ་མོས་བྱེད་ནས |
| always | *tâgpar* | རྟག་པར |
| amazing | *hâlay-pa* | ཧ་ལས་པ |
| ambassador | *shung-tshâp* | གཞུང་ཚབ |

VOCABULARY

| among | *nâng-nay* | ནང་ནས་ |
| ancient | *nâ-ngamo* | གནའ་སྔ་མོ་ |
| and | *tâng* | དང་ |
| angry | *lung-lângpo* | རླུང་ལང་པོ་ |
| answer | *len* | ལན་ |
| antique | *nga-mo* | སྔ་མོའི་ |
| any | *kâray yinay* | ག་རེ་ཡིན་ནའང་ |
| anything | *ka-yâng* | གང་ཡང་ |
| anytime | *kâdü yinay-yâng* | ག་དུས་ཡིན་ནའང་ |
| anywhere | *kâba yinay-yâng* | ག་པར་ཡིན་ནའང་ |
| appointment | *dzom-dü* | འཛོམས་དུས་ |
| approximately | *hâlam* | ཧ་ལམ་ |
| archaeological | *na-ngola tâgpay rignay* | གནའ་རྡོལ་ལ་བརྟགས་<br>པའི་རིགས་གནས་ |
| argue | *tsöpa gyâb* | རྩོད་པ་བརྒྱབ་ |
| argument | *tsöpa* | རྩོད་པ་ |
| arrive | *jorpa* | འབྱོར་པ་ |
| art | *lâg-tsal* | ལག་རྩལ་ |
| ask | *kaycha driy-wa/ lâp-pa* | སྐད་ཆ་དྲི་བ/ལབ་པ་ |
| ashtray | *tama dhâb-sa* | ཐ་མ་དབབ་ས་ |
| asleep | *nyi-koogpa* | གཉིད་ཁུགས་པ་ |
| aspirin | *gawmen aspirin* | མགོ་སྨན་ཨེ་སི་པི་རིན་ |
| at | *triy-la/la* | འཁྲིས་ལ/ལ་ |
| automatic | *râng-gul* | རང་འགུལ་ |

## B

| | | |
|---|---|---|
| baby | *pugu* | ཕུ་གུ |
| babysitter | *pugu ta-kyen/ bu-dzi* | ཕུ་གུ་བལྟ་མཁན/བུ་རྫི |
| backpack | *gya-phay* | རྒྱབ་ཕད/རྒྱབ་ལྟར |
| bad | *dukcha* | སྡུག་ཆགས |
| bag | *bag-la/jola* | འབག་ལ/ཇོ་ལ |
| baggage | *tog-tray* | དོག་ཏྲེས |
| ball | *polo* | པོ་ལོ |
| bank | *ngü-khâng* | དངུལ་ཁང |
| bar | *châng-khâng* | ཆང་ཁང |
| barbeque | *me-tâg* | མེ་བཏག |
| bathroom | *trü-khâng* | ཁྲུས་ཁང |
| battery (car) | *motay log-men* | མོ་ཊའི་གློག་སྨན |
| battery (radio, etc) | *log-shu-men (lung-tin)* | གློག་ཤུ་སྨན (རླུང་འཕྲིན་སོགས) |
| beach | *tsho-dâm chetâng* | མཚོ་འགྲམ་བྱེ་ཐང |
| beautiful | *nying jepo* | སྙིང་རྗེ་པོ |
| because | *kâng-yin sayna* | གང་ཡིན་ཟེར་ན |
| bed | *nyel-tiy* | ཉལ་ཁྲི |
| bedbugs | *dri-shig* | འདྲེ་ཤིག |
| before | *ngön-la* | སྔོན་ལ |
| beggar | *trâng-po* | སྤྲང་པོ |
| begin | *gon-dzug* | འགོ་བཙུགས |
| beginner | *go-dzuken/ lay tâng-po* | འགོ་བཙུགས་མཁན/ལས་དང་པོ |
| behind | *gyâb-la/jela* | རྒྱབ་ལ/ཇེ་ལ |

| | | |
|---|---|---|
| below | *ogla* | དོག་ལ |
| bent/crooked | *goog-kyog* | གུག་བཀྱོག |
| beside | *tri-la* | འཁྲིས་ལ |
| best | *yâg-shö* | ཡག་ཤོས |
| better | *yâgpa* | ཡག་པ |
| between | *barla* | བར་ལ |
| bicycle | *kâng gariy* | ཀང་སྒྲ་རི |
| big | *chembo* | ཆེན་པོ |
| bill (account) | *ngü-tsiy* | དངུལ་རྩིས |
| birthday | *kye-tse* | སྐྱེས་ཚེས |
| bite (n) | *so-gyâbpa/mug-pa* | སོ་བརྒྱབ་པ / རྨུག་པ |
| bitter | *khâg-tiy* | ཁག་ཏིག |
| black | *nâgbo* | ནག་པོ |
| blame | *ka-nyay gelwa* | ཁ་ཉེས་འགེལ་བ |
| blanket | *nye chay/kâmbaliy* | ཉལ་ཆས / ཀམ་བ་ལི |
| bless (v) | *jin-giy lâb* | བྱིན་གྱིས་བརླབ |
| blind | *longwa/shar-wa* | ལོང་བ / ཤར་བ |
| boat | *dru* | གྲུ |
| boil | *khö-pa/chu-tsö* | ཁོལ་པ / ཆུ་བཙོ |
| book (n) | *teb* | དེབ |
| book (v) | *teb-kyel* | དེབ་སྐྱེལ |
| bookshop | *teb tshong-khâng* | དེབ་ཚོང་ཁང |
| bored | *nyob-pa* | ཉོབས་པ |
|   I·am bored. | *nga nyop-kiy du* | ང་ཉོབས་ཀྱི་འདུག |
| borrow | *yar-wa* | གཡར་བ |
| boss | *pönpo* | དཔོན་པོ |

| both | *nyi-ga* | གཉིས་ཀ |
| bottle | *shetâm* | ཤེལ་དམ |
| bottle opener | *shetâm kha-cheyâk* | ཤེལ་དམ་ཁ་ཕྱེ་ཡག |
| box | *gâm* | སྒྲོམ |
| boy | *bu* | བུ |
| boyfriend | *togpo* | གྲོགས་པོ |
| bracelet | *lâg-doob* | ལག་གདུབ |
| brave | *pa-o* | དཔའ་པོ |
| break | *châg-pa* | གཅོག་པ |
| breakfast | *shokay khala* | ཞོགས་ཀའི་ཁ་ལག |
| bribe (n) | *kog-nyan taypa* | སྐྱོག་རྫས |
| bribe (v) | *kog-nyan tay* | སྐྱོག་རྫས་སྤྲད་པ |
| bridge | *sâmpa* | ཟམ་པ |
| bright | *wö-chenpo* | འོད་ཅན་པོ |
| bring | *kyer-wa/tri-pa* | བསྐྱུར་བ/འཁྲིད་པ |
| broken | *châg-pa* | བཅག་པ |
| building | *khâng-pa* | ཁང་པ |
| burn (v) | *tshig-pa* | འཚིག་པ |
| bus | *ba-say/dru-kye lângkhor/mota* | བསབ་སེ/འགྲུལ་སྐྱེལ་རླངས་འཁོར་མོ་ཊ |
| business | *tshong* | ཚོང |
| busy | *tewa* | བྲེལ་བ |
| but | *yi-nay yâng* | ཨིན་ནའང |
| buy | *nyo-wa* | ཉོ་བ |
| by | *tsala/goh-nay* | རྩ་ལ/སྒོ་ནས |

VOCABULARY

## C

| | | |
|---|---|---|
| cafe | *sakhâng* | ཟ་ཁང་ |
| camera | *parchay* | པར་ཆས་ |
| camp (v) | *gur gyâb/gar gyâb* | གུར་བརྒྱབ།/གར་བརྒྱབ་པ་ |
| I am camping. | *nga gur gyâb-nay tay yö* | ང་གུར་བརྒྱབ་ནས་བསྡད་ཡོད། |
| camp (n) | *gar* | སྒར་ |
| can | *châgtin* | ཆུགས་ཏིན་ |
| can opener | *châgtin kha-cheyak* | ཆུགས་ཏིན་ཁ་ཕྱེ་ཡག་ |
| candle | *yâng-la* | ཡང་ལ་ |
| capitalism | *mâtsay ringlu* | མ་རྩའི་རིང་ལུགས་ |
| car | *mota* | མོ་ཊ་ |
| cards (playing) | *ta-siy* | ད་སི་ |
| care (to take care of) | *da-nyer jepa* | བདག་གཉེར་བྱེད་པ་ |
| careful | *sâp-sâp* | ཟབ་ཟབ་ |
| carry | *kyer-wa* | བཀྱེར་བ་ |
| cashier | *ngü-nyer* | དངུལ་གཉེར་ |
| cemetery | *dü-trü* | དུར་ཁྲོད་ |
| certain | *ngay-pa* | ངེས་པ་ |
| chance | *tâb-digpa* | སྟབས་འགྲིགས་པ་ |
| chair | *kup-kyâg* | རྐུབ་ཀྱག་ |
| change (coins) | *ngü-silma* | དངུལ་སིལ་མ་ |
| change (trains) | *jepo* | བརྗེ་པོ/བརྒྱུར་བ་ |
| cheap | *kay-po* | ཁེ་པོ་ |
| chemist (pharmacy) | *men tshong-khâng* | སྨན་ཚོང་ཁང་ |

| | | |
|---|---|---|
| child | pugu | ཕྲུ་གུ |
| choose (vb) | dhem-pa | འདེམས་པ |
| cigarettes | thama | ཐ་མག |
| cigarette papers | thama shugu | ཐ་མག་ཤོག་གུ |
| city (centre) | drong-kay (kyil) | གྲོང་ཁྱེར་དཀྱིལ |
| clean | tsâng-ma | གཙང་མ |
| close (adj) | triy-la/drâm-la | འཁྲིས་ལ/འགྲམ་ལ |
| coat | tö dung | སྟོད་དུང |
| cold | trâng-mo | གྲང་མོ |
| come | lebpa/jorpa/ yongwa | ཡོང་བ/སླེབས་པ/འབྱོར་བ |
| comfortable | kyipo/depo | བདེ་པོ/སྐྱིད་པོ |
| communism | marpö ringlu | དམར་པོའི་རིང་ལུགས |
| company (friend) | rogpa | རོགས་པ |
| company (business) | tshong-lay | ཚོང་ལས |
| complex (confusing) | gaw nyog-po | མགོ་རྙོག་པོ |
| condom | lig-shup | རྟིག་ཤུབས |
| Congratulations! | tashidelek | བཀྲ་ཤིས་བདེ་ལེགས |
| contact lens | mig-nâng koshel | མིག་ནང་ཀོ་ཤེལ |
| contagious | gö-lâpo | འགོས་སླ་པོ |
| contraceptive | kyegaw kâyak | སྐྱེ་འགོག་ཁག་ལག |
| conversation | kaycha/ka-mol | སྐད་ཆ/ཁ་མོལ |
| cook (v) | kalâg sowa | ཁ་ལག་བཟོ་བ |
| cooperative | nyâm-lay | མཉམ་ལས |
| corner | sur | ཟུར |

|  |  |  |
|---|---|---|
| corruption | ma-wöpay gyu-ngan sayak layka | མ་འོས་པའི་རྒྱུ་ངན་ཟ་ཡག་ལས་ཀ |
| count (v) | tsiwa | རྩི་བ |
| courtyard | gawra | སྒོར |
| cramp | nya gyurwa/chüpa | ཉ་འགྱུར་བ/འཁྱུས་པ |
| crampons (lit. a hooked metal thing to climb mountains and hills) | ri dâng kadung dzeg-chay chag goog-goog | རི་དང་ཀ་དུང་འཛེགས་ཆེད་ ལྕགས་གུག་གུག་ཅིག |
| crazy | nyön-pa | སྨྱོན་པ |
| credit card | ngü-tshab lagkay | དངུལ་ཚབ་ལག་ཁྱེར |
| crop | tön-day/lotog | ལོ་ཏོག |
| crowded | tshâng-ga | འཚང་ག |
| cry | ngü-pa | དུས་པ |
| customs (officials) | go-trel lekung | སྒོ་ཁྲལ་ལས་ཁུངས |
| cut (v) | tub-pa/chaypa | གཏུབ་པ/བཅད་པ |

## D

|  |  |  |
|---|---|---|
| daily | nyin-ta | ཉིན་ལྟར |
| damp | lönpa | རློན་པ |
| dance | shâb-dro | ཞབས་བྲོ |
| dangerous | nyan-ga | ཉེན་ག |
| dark | nâgu | ནག་ཁུང |
| date (time) | tshe-pa | ཚེས་པ |
| dawn | nâm-lângdü | ནམ་ལངས |
| day | nyin-ma | ཉིན་མ |

| | | |
|---|---|---|
| dead | *shi-pa* | ཤི་པ |
| deaf | *wön-pa* | འོན་པ |
| death | *chiwa* | འཆི་བ |
| decide | *tâgchay* | ཐག་བཅད |
| decision | *tâgchö* | ཐག་གཅོད |
| delicious | *shimpo* | ཞིམ་པོ |
| delightful | *gawpo* | དགའ་པོ |
| delirious | *sem-tug chenpo* | སེམས་འཁྲུགས་ཆེན་པོ |
| democracy | *mâng-tso ringlu* | དམངས་གཙོའི་རིང་ལུགས |
| demonstration (protest) | *ngâm-tön tromkor* | ངམ་སྟོན་འཁོམས་སྐོར |
| deny | *ngo-len majehpa* | ངོ་ལེན་མ་བྱས་པ |
| depart | *thön-pa* | ཐོན་པ |
| departure | *thön-yak* | ཐོན་ཡག |
| desert | *je-thâng* | བྱེ་ཐང |
| destroy | *mepa sowa/shigpa* | མེད་པ་བཟོ་བ |
| detail | *shipta* | ཞིབ་ཕྲ |
| development | *yar-gyay* | ཡར་རྒྱས |
| dictatorship | *si-wâng gayzin* | སྲིད་དབང་སྒེར་འཛིན |
| dictionary | *tshing-dzö* | ཚིག་མཛོད |
| different | *minda-wa* | མི་འདྲ་བ |
| difficult | *khâg-po* | ཁག་པོ |
| dinner | *gawnda khala* | དགོང་དག་ཁ་ལག |
| direct | *ka-dug* | ཁ་ཐུག |
| dirt | *tsogba* | བཙོག་པ |
| dirty | *tsogba-chen* | བཙོག་པ་ཅན |

| | | |
|---|---|---|
| disadvantage | *kyön* | སྐྱོན་ |
| discount | *gong châgpa* | གོང་བཅག་པ་ |
| discover | *nyay-pa* | རྙེད་པ་ |
| discrimination | *yen-je/ten-kyer* | དབྱེ་འབྱེད་ |
| disinfectant | *duk-nyen gokmen* | དུག་ཉེན་འགོག་སྨན་ |
| distant | *tâg-gyâng* | ཐག་རྒྱང་ |
| doctor | *âmchi* | ཨེམ་ཆི་ |
| dole | *sem kyowa* | སེམས་སྐྱོ་བ་ |
| doll | *â-lay pekok* | ཨ་ལགས་པད་ཀོག་ |
| dope | *nyay-tâg* | ཉལ་ཐག་ |
| double | *nyi-tsâg/nyi-dâb* | ཉིས་ཚེགས་/ཉིས་ལྡབ་ |
| down | *wog/mar* | འོག་/མར་ |
| downstairs | *shö* | ཤོད་ |
| dream (n) | *min-lâm* | རྨི་ལམ་ |
| dried | *kâm-pa* | སྐམས་པ་ |
| drink (n) | *tung-wa* | འཐུང་བ་ |
| drink (v) | *tung* | འཐུང་ |
| drinkable (water) | *tung nyen-pa (chu)* | འཐུང་ཉན་པ་ (ཆུ་) |
| drugs | *men* | སྨན་ |
| drunk (inebriated) | *ra ziwa* | ར་བཟི་བ་ |
| dry | *kâmpo* | སྐམ་པོ་ |
| during | *kâb-la/ring-la* | རིང་ལ་ |
| dust | *thelwa* | ཐལ་བ་ |

## E

| | | |
|---|---|---|
| each | *reray* | རེ་རེ་ |
| early | *nga-po* | སྔ་པོ་ |

| | | |
|---|---|---|
| earn | *sogpa/râgpa* | གསོག་པ/རག་པ |
| earnings | *yong-bâb* | ཡོང་འབབ |
| Earth | *sa* | ས |
| earthquake | *sa-yom* | ས་འོམ |
| easy | *lay lâpo* | ལས་སླ་པོ |
| eat | *sa* | ཟ་བ |
| economical | *drosong chung-chung* | འགྲོ་སོང་ཆུང་ཆུང |
| economy | *paljor* | དཔལ་འབྱོར |
| education | *sheyön/lob-jong* | ཤེས་ཡོན/སློབ་སྦྱོང |
| elder | *ganpa* | རྒན་པ |
| election | *wö-du/wö-shog* | འོས་བསྡུ/འོས་ཤོག |
| electricity | *log* | གློག |
| elevator (lift) | *log-giy kenza* | གློག་གི་སྐས་འཛེགས |
| embarrassment | *ngo tsawa* | ངོ་ཚ་བ |
| embassy | *shung-tsâp* | གཞུང་ཚབ |
| employer | *layka tro-kyen* | ལས་ཀ་སྤྲོད་མཁན |
| empty | *tongpa* | སྟོང་པ |
| end | *ta-jug* | མཐའ་མཇུག |
| energy | *nüshug* | ནུས་ཤུགས |
| English | *injiy* | དབྱིན་ཇི |
| enjoy (oneself) | *(râng)kyipo tong* | སྐྱིད་པོ་གཏོང |
| enough | *dig-pa* | འགྲིག་པ |
| enter | *nâng-la dzüpa* | ནང་ལ་འཛུལ་པ |
| entry | *nâng-la dzüyak* | ནང་འཛུལ |
| equal | *da-nyâm* | འདྲ་མཉམ |
| evening | *gongda* | དགོང་དག |

| event | *dü-kâp* | དུས་སྐབས་ |
| every | *tshâng-ma* | ཚང་མ་ |
| every day | *nyin-ray* | ཉིན་རེ་ |
| everyone | *mi tshâng-ma* | མི་ཚང་མ་ |
| everything | *chalâg tshâng-ma* | ཅ་ལག་ཚང་མ་ |
| exchange (vb) | *jeba* | བརྗེ་བ་ |
| exhausted | *thâng chay-pa* | ཐང་ཆད་པ་ |
| exile | *kyâb-chol* | སྐྱབས་བཅོལ་ |
| exotic | *rângiy lung-par madârwa/ ya-tsenpo* | རང་གི་ལུང་པར་མ་དར་བ་/ཨ་མཚར་པོ་ |
| expensive | *gong chenpo* | གོང་ཆེན་པོ་ |
| experience | *nyâm-nyong* | ཉམས་མྱོང་ |
| export (v) | *chi-tsong jaypa* | ཕྱིར་ཚོང་བྱེད་པ་ |

## F

| false | *dzün-ma* | རྫུས་མ་ |
| family | *mi-tshâng* | མི་ཚང་ |
| fan | *lung-khor* | རླུང་འཁོར་ |
| far | *ta-ringpo* | ཐག་རིང་པོ་ |
| farm | *shin-ga* | ཞིང་ག་ |
| fast (not eating) | *say-chö* | ཟས་གཅོད་ |
| fast (quick) | *gyok-po* | མགྱོགས་པོ་ |
| fat | *gyâk-pa* | རྒྱགས་པ་ |
| fault | *non-trül* | ནོར་འཁྲུལ་ |
| my fault | *ngay non-trül* | ང་རི་ནོར་འཁྲུལ་ |
| fear | *shay-nâng* | ཞེད་སྣང་ |

| | | |
|---|---|---|
| fee | *la* | ལ་ |
| feel (v) | *tshor-wa* | ཚོར་བ་ |
| feeling | *tshor-wa* | ཚོར་བ་ |
| female | *mo* | མོ་ |
| ferry | *dru-nâng droyak* | གྲུ་ནང་འགྲོ་བ་ |
| festival | *dü-chen* | དུས་ཆེན་ |
| fever | *tsha-wa* | ཚ་བ་ |
| few | *nyung-shay* | ཉུང་ཤས་ |
| fiancé/e | *châng-sa gyâya-kiy dzâdog* | ཆང་ས་རྒྱག་ཡག་གི་མཛའ་གྲོགས་ |
| fight (n) | *gya-day* | རྒྱུ་འདེ་ |
| film (movie) | *log-nyen* | གློག་བརྙན་ |
| film (roll of) | *phing-sho* | པར་གྱི་ཤིང་ཤོག་ |
| find (v) | *nyay-pa* | བརྙེས་པ་ |
| fine (penalty) | *nye-pa* | ཉེས་པ་ |
| fire | *me* | མེ་ |
| firewood | *me-shing* | མེ་ཤིང་ |
| first | *tâng-po* | དང་པོ་ |
| flag | *darchog* | དར་ཆོག་ |
| flashlight (torch) | *logshu/bijili* | གློག་གཤུ་/བི་ཅི་ལི་ |
| flight | *nâmdu droyak* | གནམ་གྲུ་འགྲོ་ཡག་ |
| flood | *chulog* | ཆུ་ལོག་ |
| floor | *sâting-gâng* | ས་གཏིང་སྐང་ |
| follow | *shoog-la yong* | གཤུག་ལ་ཡོང་ |
| food | *khala* | ཁ་ལག་ |
| food poisoning | *say-dhug* | ཟས་དུག་ |

| | | |
|---|---|---|
| for | *döntag-la* | དོན་དག་ལ་ |
| foreign | *chigyal* | ཕྱི་རྒྱལ་ |
| forever | *tâgtu* | རྟག་ཏུ་ |
| forget (v) | *jay-pa* | བརྗེད་པ་ |
|   I forgot. | *ngay jay-song* | ངས་བརྗེད་སོང་ |
|   You forgot. | *kayrâng-giy jay-du* | ཁྱེད་རང་གིས་བརྗེད་འདུག |
| forgive | *söpa gom* | བཟོད་པ་སྒོམ་ |
| formal | *lug-sol tar* | ལུགས་སོལ་ལྟར་ |
| fragile | *châg chog-chog* | ཆག་ཆོག་ཆོག |
| free (of charge) | *rin maypa* | རིན་མེད་པ་ |
| free (not bound ) | *râng-wâng* | རང་དབང་ |
| freeze | *kyâg-pa châg* | འཁྱགས་པ་ཆགས་ |
| fresh (not stale) | *söpa* | སོས་པ་ |
| fried | *ngö-pa* | བརྔོས་པ་ |
| friend | *drogpo*(m)/<br>*drogmo*(f) | གྲོགས་པོ/གྲོགས་མོ |
| friendly | *thunpö/gawpö* | མཐུན་པོ/དགའ་པོ |
| from | *nay* | ནས་ |
| fruit | *shing-tog* | ཤིང་ཏོག |
| full | *kheng-pa* | ཁེངས་པ་ |
| fun | *nângwa kyikyi* | སྣང་བ་སྐྱིད་སྐྱིད་ |
| funny | *ken-tshar-po* | ཁྱད་མཚར་པོ་ |
| funny (person) | *tenshi tshar-po* | བརྟན་ཤིག་མཚར་པོ་ |

## G

| | | |
|---|---|---|
| game | *tsemo* | རྩེད་མོ་ |
| garbage | *gay-nyig* | གད་སྙིགས་ |

| | | |
|---|---|---|
| garden | *dhumra* | ཞུམ་ར |
| gas | *dulâng* | དུག་རྡངས |
| gas cartridge/ cylinder | *dulâng lugnö* | དུག་རྡངས་ལུགསྣོད |
| gate | *go* | སྒོ |
| generous | *lâgpa shângpo* | ལག་པ་ཤོགས་པོ |
| girl | *bumo* | བུ་མོ |
| girlfriend | *togmo* | གྲོགས་མོ |
| give | *taywa* | སྤྲེར་བ/སྐུར་བ |
| Give me ... | *nga-ła ... tay tâng* | ང་ལ ..... སྤྲད་དང |
| I'll give you ... | *ngay kayrâng-la ... tay-giy yin* | ངས་ཁྱེད་རང་ལ ..... སྤྲད་ཀྱི་ཡིན |
| glass (of water) | *chu galasiy gâng* | ཆུ་སྐལ་ལ་སི་གང |
| glasses | *mig-shay* | མིག་ཤེལ |
| go | *dro* | འགྲོ |
| I am going to ... | *nga ... -la dro-giy yin* | ང ..... ལ་འགྲོ་གི་ཡིན |
| god | *könchok* | དཀོན་མཆོག |
| gold | *say* | གསེར |
| good | *yakpo* | ཡག་པོ |
| government | *shung* | གཞུང |
| greedy | *dhöpa chenpo* | འདོད་པ་ཆེན་པོ |
| grow (v) | *gyepa* | རྒྱས་པ |
| guess (v) | *tshö-pagpa* | ཚོད་དཔག་པ |
| guide (n) | *lâmgyü chay-khen* | ལམ་སྟོན |
| guidebook | *lâmtön-teb* | ལམ་སྟོན་དེབ |

| | | |
|---|---|---|
| guilty | nye-chen/nâg-nye phogpa | ཉེས་ཅན་/ནག་ཉེས་ཕོག་པ་ |
| guitar | da-nyan/piwang | སྒྲ་སྙན་/པི་ཝང་ |

## H

| | | |
|---|---|---|
| half | chekâ | ཕྱེད་ཀ་ |
| handbag | lâgpar keyak bagla | ལག་པར་ཁྱེར་ལག་འབགླ་ |
| handicrafts | lag-shay | ལག་ཤེས་ |
| handsome | dzay-po | མཛེས་པོ་ |
| happy | kiybu | སྐྱིད་པོ་ |
| hard (object) | trâg-po | མཁྲེགས་པོ་ |
| hate | gawpo may-pa/ dâng-wa | དགའ་པོ་མེད་པ་/ཞང་བ་ |
| have (v) | yaw | ཡོད་ |
| I have ... | nga-la ... yo | ང་ལ་ — ཡོད་ |
| You have ... | kayrâng-la ... du | ཁྱེད་རང་ལ་ — འདུག་ |
| Have you (got) ...? | kayrang-la ... yaw-pay? | ཁྱེད་རང་ལ་ — ཡོད་པས་ |
| health | tröten | བཞོད་བསྟེན་ |
| hear | töpa | ཐོས་པ་ |
| heat | tsha-wa | ཚ་བ་ |
| heater | tsha-log | ཚ་སྒྲོག་ |
| heavy | jiy-kog | ཇིད་ཁོག་ |
| help (v) | rog jay-pa | རོགས་བྱེད་པ་ |
| here | day | འདིར་ |
| high | thopo | མཐོ་པོ་ |
| hill | ri | རི་ |

| | | |
|---|---|---|
| hire | *yarwa* | གཡར་བ |
| I'd like to hire it. | *nga dey yar-dö yö* | ང་གཡར་འདོད་ཡོད། |
| hitchhike | *tepo tennay drü-shu chepa* | མཐེ་བོ་བསྟན་ནས་འགྲུལ་བཞུད་བྱེད་པ |
| holiday | *gung-sâng* | གུང་སེང |
| holy | *tsa chenpo* | རྩ་ཆེན་པོ |
| home | *nâng* | ནང |
| homeland | *pha-yul* | ཕ་ཡུལ |
| homesick | *nâng drenpa* | ནང་དྲན་པ |
| homosexual | *phö phola châgpa chepa* | ཕོ་ཕོ་ལ་ཆགས་པ་བྱེད་པ |
| honest | *trâng-po* | དྲང་པོ |
| hope | *rewa* | རེ་བ |
| hospitality | *nay-len* | སྣེ་ལེན |
| hot | *tsha-bo* | ཚ་བོ |
| hotel | *dru-khâng* | འགྲུལ་ཁང |
| house | *khâng-pa* | ཁང་པ |
| housework | *nâng-lay* | ནང་ལས |
| how | *kân-te-siy* | གང་འདྲ་སེ |
| human | *mi* | མི |
| hungry (to be) | *drokok togpa* | གྲོད་ཁོག་སྟོག་པ |
| I'm hungry. | *nga drokog togiy du* | ང་གྲོད་ཁོག་སྟོག་གི་འདུག |
| Are you hungry? | *kayrâng drokok togiy dukay?* | ཁྱེད་རང་གྲོད་ཁོག་སྟོག་གི་འདུག་གས |
| hurry (to be in a) | *tewa/gyog-po* | བྲེལ་བ/མགྱོགས་པོ |
| I'm in a hurry. | *nga taywa yö* | ང་བྲེལ་བ་ཡོད། |

VOCABULARY

| hurt | naza tongwa | ནཚ་གཏོང་བ |
| husband | kyoga | ཁྱོག |
| hypnotism (make others do things in a sleep-like state) | nyi tabö-nâng lay che-choogpay rigpa | གཉིད་ལྟ་བུ་བཟུར་ལས་བྱེད་བཅུག་པའི་ རིག་པ |

## I

| ice | kyâgpa | འཁྱགས་པ |
| idea | sâmlo/rigpa | བསམ་བློ/རིག་པ |
| identification | ngo-tö | ངོ་སྤྲོད |
| if | kel-tey | གལ་ཏེ |
| ill | nawa | ན་བ |
| illegal | trim-gal | ཁྲིམས་འགལ |
| imagination | nâng-wa/mig-nâm | སྣང་བ/དམིགས་སྣང |
| immediately | lâm-sâng | ལམ་སང |
| imitation | len-dö | ལད་ཟློས |
| import (v) | nâng-dren tshong | ནང་འདྲེན་ཚོང |
| impossible | misi-pa | མི་སྲིད་པ |
| imprisonment | tsön-jug | བཙོན་འཇུག |
| in | nâng-la | ནང་ལ |
| included | nâng-tshü | ནང་ཚུད |
| inconvenient | tâb depo maypa | སྟབས་བདེ་པོ་མེད་པ |
| indoors | khâng-pay nângla | ཁང་པའི་ནང་ལ |
| industry | so-dra | བཟོ་གྲྭ |
| infection | gö-nay | འགོས་ནད |
| infectious | gönay-chen | འགོས་ནད་ཅན |

| | | |
|---|---|---|
| informal | *lugtün migaw-pa* | ལུགས་བསྟུན་མི་དགོས་པ |
| information | *nay-tsül* | གནས་ཚུལ |
| injection | *men-kâp* | སྨན་ཁབ |
| injury | *may-kyön* | རྨས་སྐྱོན |
| insect repellant | *du-drâng kayak-men* | དུག་སྦྲང་བཀག་འགོག་ལགས་སྨན |
| inside | *nâng-la* | ནང་ལ |
| instant | *kyug-tsâm* | སྐྱུག་ཙམ |
| insurance | *nye-sung ganlen* | ཉེན་སྲུང་བལན་ལེན |
| insure (v) | *nye-sung ganlen chepa* | ཉེན་སྲུང་བལན་ལེན་བྱེད་པ |
| It's insured. | *dey-la ngan-sung ganlen yö* | དེ་ལ་ངན་སྲུང་བལན་ལེན་བྱེད་ཡོད |
| intelligent | *rigpa yakpo* | རིག་པ་ཡག་པོ |
| interested | *ying yöpa* | དབྱིངས་ཡོད་པ |
| interesting | *nyen-po* | སྙན་པོ |
| international | *gya-chiy* | རྒྱལ་སྤྱི |
| invite (v) | *kay tângwa* | སྐད་བཏང་བ |
| itch | *sâb-ra lângwa* | ཟབ་ར་ལངས་བ |

## J

| | | |
|---|---|---|
| jail (gaol) | *tsön-khâng* | བཙོན་ཁང |
| jazz | *jaz rocha* | ཇཛ་རོ་ཙ |
| jeans | *jiynz* | ཇིན |
| jewellery | *gen-jâ* | རྒྱན་ཆ |
| job | *layka* | ལས་ཀ |
| joke (n) | *tenshi longwa* | བཞད་གད་ཤོད་པ |
| justice | *trâng-ten* | དྲང་བདེན |

## K

| | | |
|---|---|---|
| key | de-miy | ལྡེའུ་མིག |
| kill | say-pa | གསོད་པ |
| kind (feeling) | sem sângpo | སེམས་བཟང་པོ |
| king | gyalpo | རྒྱལ་པོ |
| kiss | kha kyewa | ཁ་བསྐྱལ་བ |
| knapsack | phay-kok | ཕད་གོག |
| know (to be acquainted with) | gyü-yö/driy-pa | རྒྱུས་ཡོད/འདྲིས་པ |
| to have knowledge of, to know how to | shay-pa | ཤེས་པ |

## L

| | | |
|---|---|---|
| lake | tsho | མཚོ |
| land | sa-cha | ས་ཆ |
| landslide | sa-gaypa/sarü | ས་གཤད་པ/ས་རུད |
| language | keyig | སྐད་ཡིག |
| last (adj) | ta-ma | མཐའ་མ |
| late | chipo | ཕྱི་པོ |
| laugh | gaymo shorwa | གད་མོ་ཤོར་བ |
| laundry | dulog tru-khâng | དུག་ལོག་འཁྲུས་ཁང |
| law | thrim | ཁྲིམས |
| lawyer | thrim tsöpa | ཁྲིམས་རྩོད་པ |
| lazy | nyob-to/laylo-chen | སྙོབ་ཏོ/ལེ་ལོ་ཅན |
| learn | jong-wa | སྦྱོང་བ |

| | | |
|---|---|---|
| left | yön | གཡོན་ |
| left-wing | yönchog shokak | གཡོན་ཕྱོགས་ཤོག་ཁག |
| legal | trim-thog | ཁྲིམས་ཐོག |
| less | nyung-wa | ཉུང་བ |
| letter | yigay | ཡི་གེ |
| liar | kyâg-dzün shoken | རྐུག་བཟུན་ཤོད་མཁན |
| lice | shig | ཤིག |
| life | tse/sog | ཚེ་/སྲོག |
| lift (elevator) | log-giy kenza | གློག་གི་སྐས་འཛེགས |
| light | log | གློག |
| lighter | may-par-yak | མེ་སྤར་ཡག |
| like (similar) | nâng-shin/dâpo | ནང་བཞིན་/འདྲ་པོ |
| like (v) | gawpo | དགའ་པོ |
| line | thig | ཐིག |
| listen | nyen-pa | ཉན་པ |
| little (adj) | chung-chung | ཆུང་ཆུང་ |
| live (v) | te-pa/sönpa | བསྡད་པ/གསོན་པ |
| lock (n) | go-châg | སྒོ་ལྕགས |
| long | ringpo | རིང་པོ |
| long ago | yün ringpo ngön-la | ཡུན་རིང་པོ་སྔོན་ལ |
| look for (v) | ta-war | བལྟ་བར |
| lose | lâhg-pa | བརླག་པ |
| lost | lâhg-pa | བརླག་པ |
| loud | kay-shug chenpo | སྐད་ཤུགས་ཆེན་པོ |
| love | gawpo/tsewa | དགའ་པོ་/རྩེ་བ |
| I love it. | nga tayla gawpo yö | ང་དེ་ལ་དགའ་པོ་ཡོད |

| I love you. | nga kayrâng-la gawpo yö | ང་ཁྱེད་རང་ལ་དགའ་པོ་ཡོད་ |
| lucky | sonâm-chen | བསོད་ནམས་ཅན |
| lunch | nyin-gung kalâg | ཉིན་གུང་ཁ་ལག |

## M

| machine | trü-khor | འཕྲུལ་འཁོར་ |
| mad (crazy) | nyön-pa | སྨྱོན་པ |
| made (to be made of) | sö-pa | བཟོས་པ |
| majority | mâng-chewa | མང་ཆེ་བ |
| make | so-wa | བཟོ་བ |
| many | mâng-po | མང་པོ |
| map | sâpta | ས་བཀྲ |
| market | trom | ཁྲོམ |
| marriage | châng-sa | ཆང་ས |
| marry | châng-sa gyâp | ཆང་ས་བརྒྱབ |
| matches (competitions) | dren-du | འགྲན་བསྡུར |
| material | gyub-ja | རྒྱུ་ཆ |
| maybe | chig chay-na | གཅིག་བྱེད་ན |
| meet | thug-tay | ཐུག་སྡད |
| I'll meet you. | nga kayrang thu-giy yin | ང་ཁྱེད་རང་ཐུག་གི་ཡིན |
| We can meet you. | nga-tso kayrang thug thup-kiy ray | ང་ཚོ་ཁྱེད་རང་ཐུག་ཐུབ་ཀྱི་རེད |

| menu | *kalâg tho* | ཁ་ལག་ཐོ |
| message | *len* | ལན |
| mind (n) | *sem* | སེམས |
| minute | *karma* | སྐར་མ |
| miss (feel absence of) | *dren pa* | དྲན་པ |
| I'll miss you. | *nga kayrâng tren-sa ray* | ང་ཁྱེད་རང་དྲན་ཟ་རེད |
| mistake | *non-trül* | ནོར་འཁྲུལ |
| mix (v) | *drepa* | འདྲེ་བ |
| modern | *teng-dü* | དེང་དུས |
| money | *ngü* | དངུལ |
| monument | *densow-ten* | དྲན་གསོའི་རྟེན |
| more | *mâng-wa* | མང་བ |
| morning | *nga-dro* | སྔ་དྲོ |
| mountain | *ri* | རི |
| mountaineering | *ri gâng-la dzâg-gyu* | རི་སྒང་ལ་འཛེག་རྒྱུ |
| movie | *log-nyen* | གློག་བརྙན |
| museum | *demton-khâng* | འགྲེམས་སྟོན་ཁང |
| music | *roja/roshay* | རོལ་གཞས |

## N

| name | *ming* | མིང |
| narcotic | *siy-men* | བཟིའི་སྨན |
| national park | *mimâng ling-ga* | རྒྱལ་ཡོངས་སྐྱེད་ཚལ་ག |
| nature | *râng-jung* | རང་བྱུང |
| near | *tri-la* | ཁྲིས་ལ |

| | | |
|---|---|---|
| necessary | *gaw ngay-chen* | དགོས་ངེས་ཅན |
| neither | *nyika minpa* | གཉིས་ཀ་མིན་པ |
| never | *tsawa-nay* | རྩ་བ་ནས |
| new | *sa-ba* | གསར་པ |
| news | *sân-gyur* | གསར་འགྱུར |
| newspaper | *tshâgba* | ཚགས་པར |
| next | *jema* | རྗེས་མ |
| nice | *yâkpo* | ཡག་པོ |
| night | *gongda* | མཚན་མོ |
| noise | *kaycho* | སྐད་ཆ |
| noisy | *kaycho tsha-po* | སྐད་ཆ་ཚ་པོ |
| none | *chig-kyâng* | གཅིག་ཀྱང |
| not any more | *ta-may/ta-min* | ད་མེད/ད་མིན |
| nothing | *ga-yâng may/ gayâng min* | གང་ཡང་མེད/ གང་ཡང་མིན |
| not yet | *tânda-yâng may/ tânda yâng min* | ད་ལྟ་ཡང་མེད/ ད་ལྟ་ཡང་མིན |
| now | *tânda* | ད་ལྟ |
| nuclear energy | *dü-tren nüpa* | རྡུལ་ཕྲན་ནུས་པ |
| nuclear-free | *dü-trent tsön-ja kâgok* | རྡུལ་ཕྲན་མཚོན་ཆ་བཀག་འགོག |

## O

| | | |
|---|---|---|
| obvious | *ngönsay töpo* | མངོན་གསལ་དོད་པོ |
| occupation | *tsho-tâb/layka* | འཚོ་ཐབས/ལས་ཀ |
| ocean | *gyâm-tsho* | རྒྱ་མཚོ |
| offend (v) | *nö-pa* | གནོད་པ |

| offer (v) | taywa | སྟེར་བ |
| office | laykung | ལས་ཁུངས |
| officer | lejay-pa | ལས་བྱེད་པ |
| often | yâng yâng/yâng-se | ཡང་ཡང་/ཡང་སེ |
| oil | noom | སྣུམ |
| old | nying-pa | རྙིང་པ |
| on | gângla | སྒང་ལ |
| once | teng-chig | ཐེང་གཅིག |
| one | chig | གཅིག |
| only | chigpo/ma-tog | གཅིག་པོ/མ་གཏོགས |
| open (v) | ka-che | ཁ་ཕྱེ |
| open (adj) | ka-cheway | ཁ་ཕྱེ་བ |
| opinion | sâm-tshül | བསམ་ཚུལ |
| opportunity | go-kâb | གོ་སྐབས |
| opposite | gal-dha | འགལ་ཟླ |
| or | yâng-na | ཡང་ན |
| order (n) | kah | བཀའ |
| ordinary | kyüma | རྒྱུས་མ |
| organisation | tshog-pa/digzug | ཚོགས་པ/སྒྲིག་འཛུགས |
| organise (v) | tâtig jaypa | སྒྲ་འབྲིགས་བྱེད་པ |
| original | ngo-ma | ངོ་མ |
| other | shenda | གཞན་དག |
| out | chi | ཕྱི |
| outside | chilog | ཕྱི་ལོག |
| over | thog-la | ཐོག་ལ |
| overnight | shâgpo-chig | ཞག་པོ་གཅིག |

| | | |
|---|---|---|
| overseas | *chigyal* | ཕྱི་རྒྱལ |
| owe (v) | *jal gawpa* | འཇལ་དགོས་པ |
| I owe you. | *ngay kayrâng-la jalgaw yo* | ངས་ཁྱེད་རང་ལ་འཇལ་དགོས་ཡོད |
| You owe me. | *kayrâng-giy ngala jalgaw ray* | ཁྱེད་རང་གིས་ང་ལ་འཇལ་དགོས་རེད |
| owner | *dâgpo* | བདག་པོ |

## P

| | | |
|---|---|---|
| package | *di-thum/gâm* | སྒྲིལ་པ་ཐུམ/སྒམ |
| pack of cigarettes | *thama gâm-chig* | ཐ་མག་སྒམ་གཅིག |
| packet | *gâm* | སྒམ |
| padlock | *go-châg* | སྒོ་ལྕགས |
| painful | *nâsug chenpo* | ན་ཟུག་ཆེན་པོ |
| pair | *cha* | ཆ |
| paper | *shugu* | ཤོག་བུ |
| parcel | *chalâg/topo* | དོ་པོ/ཅ་ལག |
| park | *ling-ga* | གླིང་ག |
| parliament | *gya-yong tö-tshog* | རྒྱལ་ཡོངས་གྲོས་ཚོགས |
| part | *cha-shay* | ཆ་ཤས |
| participate (v) | *shoog* | གཞུགས |
| participation | *shoog-pa* | ཞུགས་པ |
| particular | *mig-su karwa* | དམིགས་སུ་དཀར་བ |
| party | *tshog-pa* | ཚོགས་པ |
| passenger | *drü-pa* | འགྲུལ་པ |
| passport | *chi thün lâg-teb* | ཕྱི་བསྐྱོད་ལག་དེབ |
| past | *day-pa/ngön-ma* | འདས་པ/སྔོན་མ |

| | | |
|---|---|---|
| path | *lâm* | ལམ |
| pay (v) | *la taypa* | ལ་སྤྲད་པ |
| peace | *shiy-de* | ཞི་བདེ |
| pen | *nyugu* | སྙུ་གུ |
| pencil | *shânyu* | ཞ་སྙུག |
| people | *mi-mùng* | མི་དམངས |
| perfect | *kyön tsânay maypa* | སྐྱོན་ཙ་ནས་མེད་པ |
| permanent | *tenchâg* | གཏན་ཚགས |
| permission | *chog-chen* | ཚོག་འཆན |
| permit (n) | *lâg-kyay* | ལག་ཁྱེར |
| persecution | *nya-nun tongwa* | གཉའ་གནོན་གཏོང་བ |
| person | *mi* | མི |
| personal | *ger* | གེར |
| personality | *shika* | གཤིས་ཀ |
| photo | *par* | པར |
| photograph (n) | *par* | པར |
| photograph (v) | *par gyâb* | པར་བརྒྱབ |
| piece | *tum-bu* | དུམ་བུ |
| place | *sacha* | ས་ཆ |
| plane | *nâmdru* | གནམ་གྲུ |
| plant | *shing-tsay/tsi-shing* | ཤིང་ཚལ/རྩི་ཤིང |
| play (v) | *tsemo tsay* | རྩེ་མོ་རྩེད |
| plenty | *mâng-po* | མང་པོ |
| point (v) | *dzup-tön jaypa* | མཛུབ་སྟོན་བྱེད་པ |
| police | *korsung-wa* | སྐོར་སྲུང་བ |
| politics | *sitön* | སྲིད་དོན |

| | | |
|---|---|---|
| pollution | *du-drip* | དུ་སྒྲིབ |
| pool (swimming) | *kal-dzing* | རྐྱལ་རྫིང |
| poor | *kyopo* | སྐྱོ་པོ |
| positive | *teng-kaypo* | གདེང་ཁེལ་པོ |
| postcard | *drâg-sho* | སྒྲག་ཤོག |
| pottery | *dza-chay* | རྫ་ཆས |
| poverty | *wü-phong* | དབུལ་འཕོངས |
| power | *nüpa/nü-shug* | ནུས་པ/ནུས་ཤུགས |
| practical | *baychö-chen* | བེད་སྤྱོད་ཅན |
| prayer | *mönlâm* | སྨོན་ལམ |
| prefer | *tâmga/gawa* | གདམ་ག/དགའ་བ |
| pregnant | *pugu kyeyak yawpa* | ཕྲུ་གུ་སྐྱེ་ཡག་ཡོད་པ |
| prepare | *ta tig-pa* | གྲ་སྒྲིག་པ |
| present (time) | *tânda* | ད་ལྟ |
| present (gift) | *ngen-pa/lâg-ta* | རྔན་པ/ལགས་རྟགས |
| president | *siy-dzin* | སྲིད་འཛིན |
| pretty | *nying-jaypo* | སྙིང་རྗེ་པོ |
| prevent | *ngön-gok chepa* | སྔོན་འགོག་བྱེད་པ |
| price | *gong* | གོང |
| priest | *lama* | བླ་མ |
| prime minister | *siy-lön* | སྲིད་བློན |
| prison | *tson-khâng* | བཙོན་ཁང |
| prisoner | *tsönpa* | བཙོན་པ |
| private | *ger* | སྒེར |
| probably | *chig chena* | གཅིག་བྱས་ན |
| problem | *nyog-ta* | ཉོག་ཐ |

| process | *sotün chay* | བཟོ་འདོན་བྱེད |
| procession | *rudig* | རུ་སྒྲིག |
| produce (v) | *sotün chay/kyepa* | བཟོ་སྐྲུན་བྱེད་པ།/སྐྱེད་པ |
| professional | *tsho-ten/layrig* | ཚོ་རྟེན།/ལས་རིགས |
| profit | *kaysâng* | ཁེ་བཟང |
| promise | *kaylen* | ཁས་ལེན་པ |
| prostitute | *shâng tsongma* | གཞུང་ཚོང་མ |
| protect | *sung-kyob chay* | སྲུང་སྐྱོབ་བྱེད |
| protest (n) | *ngo-göl* | ངོ་རྒོལ |
| public | *chipay* | སྤྱི་པའི |
| pull | *tenpa/drü-pa* | འཐེན་པ།/དྲུད་པ |
| push | *bhu-kya gyâp* | སྤུ་རྒྱག་བརྒྱབ |

## Q

| quality | *püka* | སྤུས་ཀ |
| question (n) | *tiwa* | དྲི་བ |
| quick | *gyokpo* | མགྱོགས་པོ |
| quiet | *ku-simpo* | ཁུ་སིམ་པོ |

## R

| race (contest) | *dren-du* | འགྲན་སྡུར |
| racist | *mirig chorig chayken* | མི་རིགས་ཕྱོགས་རིས་བྱེད་མཁན |
| radio | *lung-trin* | རླུང་འཕྲིན |
| railway | *riliy châglâm* | རི་ལིའི་ལྕགས་ལམ |
| rain | *charpa* | ཆར་པ |
| raining | *charpa bâb* | ཆར་པ་བབས |

| | | |
|---|---|---|
| rape (n) | *tsen-wâng thog châgpa chöpa* | བཙན་དབང་ཐོག་ཆགས་པ་སྤྱོད་པ |
| rape (v) | *tsen-wang tog chagpa chö* | བཙན་དབང་ཐོག་ཆགས་པ་སྤྱོད |
| rare | *könpo* | དཀོན་པོ |
| raw | *jenpa* | རྗེན་པ |
| ready | *chog-chog* | ཚོག་ཚོག |
| reason | *gyum-tshen* | རྒྱུ་མཚན |
| receipt | *chung-dzin* | བྱུང་འཛིན |
| recently | *nye-cha* | ཉེ་ཆར |
| recommend | *gyâb-nün chay* | རྒྱབ་སྣོན་བྱེད |
| refugee | *kyâb-cho-wa* | སྐྱབས་འཚོལ་བ |
| refund | *chilog chay* | ཕྱིར་ལོག་བྱེད |
| refuse | *kay malâng* | ཁས་མ་བླངས |
| region | *sa-kül* | ས་ཁུལ |
| regulation | *dig-trim* | སྒྲིག་ཁྲིམས |
| relation | *delwa* | འབྲེལ་བ |
| relationship | *nye-del* | ཉེ་འབྲེལ |
| relax | *lhö-lhö* | ལྷོད་ལྷོད |
| religion | *chö-lug* | ཆོས་ལུགས |
| remember | *drenpa* | དྲན་པ |
| remote | *lung-kug/takob* | ལུང་ཁུག/ མཐའ་འཁོབ |
| rent (n) | *yarla* | གཡར་ལ |
| rent (v) | *yar* | གཡར |
| representative | *thu-miy* | འཐུས་མི |
| republic | *chithün gyakâb* | སྤྱི་མཐུན་རྒྱལ་ཁབ |

| | | |
|---|---|---|
| reservation | *ngön-nay tenkal chaypa* | སྔོན་ནས་གཏན་འཁེལ་བྱེད་པ |
| reserve (v) | *ngön-nay tenkal chay* | སྔོན་ནས་གཏན་འཁེལ་བྱེད |
| respect (n) | *gü-shâp/tsi-jog* | གུས་ཞབས/རྩི་འཇོག |
| responsibility | *lay-gan* | ལས་འགན |
| rest | *ngalso-gyâb* | ངལ་གསོ་རྒྱབ |
| restaurant | *sakhâng* | ཟ་ཁང |
| return (v) | *tshu-logpa* | ཚུར་ལོག་པ |
| revolution | *sar-je* | གསར་བརྗེ |
| rich | *chug-po* | ཕྱུག་པོ |
| right (opposite of left) | *yay* | གཡས |
| right (not wrong) | *dhen-pa/tâg-tâg* | བདེན་པ/དྲག་དྲག |
| I'm right. | *nga tâg-tâg ray* | ང་དྲག་དྲག་རེད |
| You're right. | *kayrâng tâg-tâg ray* | ཁྱེད་རང་དྲག་དྲག་རེད |
| right-wing | *yay-chog shokak* | གཡས་ཕྱོགས་ཤོག་ཁག |
| risk | *nyen-ga* | ཉེན་ག |
| road | *lâm-ga* | ལམ་ག |
| robber | *châg-pa* | ཆག་པ |
| robbery | *trog-chom* | འཕྲོག་བཅོམ |
| roof | *to-kha* | ཐོག་ཁ |
| room | *khâng-pa* | ཁང་པ |
| rope | *tâgpa* | ཐག་པ |
| round | *gogor* | སྒོར་སྒོར |
| rubbish | *kay-nyig* | གད་སྙིགས |

| | | |
|---|---|---|
| ruins | *shig-rü* | ཞིག་རལ |
| rule | *wâng-gyur jay* | དབང་སྒྱུར་བྱེད |

## S

| | | |
|---|---|---|
| sad | *sem kyowa* | སེམས་སྐྱོ་བ |
| safe (n) | *nyen-ga maypa* | ཉེན་ག་མེད་པ |
| safe (adj) | *nyen-ga mepay* | ཉེན་ག་མེད་པའི |
| safety | *nyen-ga may-gyü* | ཉེན་ག་མེད་རྒྱུ |
| salty | *tsha-ku* | ཚ་ཁུ |
| same | *chig-pa* | གཅིག་པ |
| save | *kyob-pa* | སྐྱོབ་པ |
| scenery | *yu-jong* | ཡུལ་ལྗོངས |
| seasick | *tso-nâng dronay shenlog gyâbpa* | མཚོ་ནང་འགྲོ་ནས་ཞེན་ལོག་བརྒྱབ་པ |
| secret | *sângwa* | གསང་བ |
| selfish | *râng-shay tsâpo* | རང་ཤེད་ཚ་པོ |
| sell | *tsong* | འཚོང |
| send | *tâng* | གཏང |
| serious | *tshâb-che* | ཚབས་ཆེ |
| several | *ka-chen/kâshay* | འགའ་ཆེན/ཁ་ཤས |
| sexist (most sexist) | *döchag cheshö* | འདོད་ཆགས་ཆེ་ཤོས |
| shade (n) | *đrib-na* | གྲིབ་ནག |
| shape | *sob-ta* | བཟོ་བཟུས |
| share | *go-sha* | བགོ་བཤའ |
| short (duration/time) | *kyuk-tsam* | ཁྱུག་ཙམ |

| | | |
|---|---|---|
| short (height) | *tung-tung* | ཐུང་ཐུང་ |
| shortage | *ma tângwa* | མ་འདང་བ་པ |
| shout (v) | *kay gyâb-pa* | སྐད་བརྒྱབ་ |
| show (v) | *tön* | སྟོན་ |
|   Show me. |   *nga-la tön da* | ང་ལ་སྟོན་དང་ |
| shut (adj) | *ka-gyâb-pa/* | ཁ་བརྒྱབ་པ/ ཁ་བཙུམས་པ |
| | *ka-tsum-pa* | |
| shut (v) | *ka-gyâb/ka-tsum* | ཁ་བརྒྱབ/ ཁ་བཙུམས |
| shy | *ngo tsha-wa* | ངོ་ཚ་བ |
| sick | *nah-wa* | ནད་པ |
| sickness | *na-tsa* | ན་ཚ |
| side | *chog/sur* | ཕྱོགས/ ཟུར |
| sign | *tâg* | རྟགས |
| silver | *ngü* | དངུལ |
| similar | *chigpa* | གཅིག་པ |
| since | *tsâng/nay* | ཙང/ ནས |
| single (unmarried) | *mi-hrâng* | མི་ཧྲང |
| sit | *dhay-pa* | བསྡད་པ |
| situation | *nay-tâng* | གནས་སྟངས |
| size | *tshay* | ཚད |
| sleep | *nyiy* | གཉིད |
| sleepy (to be) | *nyiy töpo* | གཉིད་བྱུང |
| slow | *kâlay/te-po* | གལེ/ དལ་པོ |
| slowly | *kâlay kâlay* | ག་ལེ་ག་ལེ |
| small | *chun-chun* | ཆུང་ཆུང |
| smell (n) | *dima* | དྲི་མ |

| | | |
|---|---|---|
| socialism | *chi-tsog ringlu* | སྤྱི་ཚོགས་རིང་ལུགས་ |
| solid | *trâg-po* | མཁྲེགས་པོ་ |
| some | *ka-shay* | ཁ་ཤས་ |
| somebody | *mi-chig* | མི་ཞིག་ |
| something | *chig* | ཅིག་ |
| sometimes | *tshâm-tshâm* | མཚམས་མཚམས་ |
| song | *lu* | གླུ་ |
| soon | *gyok-po* | མགྱོགས་པོ་ |
| sorry (I am) | *(ngay) gong-da* | (ངས་) དགོངས་དག |
| souvenir | *dren-ten* | དྲན་རྟེན་ |
| special | *migsel* | དམིགས་བསལ་ |
| sport | *lü-tsel* | ལུས་རྩལ་ |
| standard | *tsay-dhen* | ཚད་ལྡན་ |
| start | *gon-dzug* | འགོ་འཛུགས་ |
| stay | *dhay-pa* | བསྡད་པ་ |
| steal | *ku-wa* | རྐུ་བ་ |
| stop (v) | *kâkpa* | བཀག་པ་ |
| story (tale) | *drung* | སྒྲུང་ |
| straight | *ka-tug* | ཁ་ཐུག |
| strange | *ken-tsâpo* | ཁྱད་མཚར་ |
| stranger | *ngo mashay-pay-miy* | ངོ་མ་ཤེས་པའི་མི་ |
| street | *lâmka* | ལམ་ཁ་ |
| strong | *shug chenpo* | ཤུགས་ཆེན་པོ་ |
| stupid | *kug-pa* | གླེན་པ་ |
| style | *jay-tâng* | བྱེད་སྟངས་ |
| suddenly | *hop-ti khala* | ཆོབ་ཏེ་ཁ་ལ་ |

| | | |
|---|---|---|
| sun | *nyin-ma* | ཉི་མ |
| sunglasses | *mig-shay napo* | མིག་ཤེལ་ནག་པོ |
| sure | *ten-ten* | གཏན་གཏན |
| surprise | *ha-laypa* | ཧ་ལས་པ |
| I'm surprised. | *nga ha lay-song* | ང་ཧ་ལས་སོང་། |
| survive | *sönpa* | གསོན་པ |
| sweet | *nga-mo* | མངར་མོ |
| swim | *kel gyâb-pa* | རྐྱལ་བརྒྱབ་པ |

## T

| | | |
|---|---|---|
| take | *lenpa* | ལེན་པ |
| talk (v) | *shay-pa* | བཤད་པ |
| tall | *ring-po* | རིང་པོ |
| tasty | *towa chenpo* | རོ་བ་ཆེན་པོ |
| tax | *tay* | ཁྲལ |
| telephone (n) | *kapa* | ཁ་པར |
| telephone (v) | *kapa tong* | ཁ་པར་གཏོང |
| telephone book | *kapa âhng-teb* | ཁ་པར་ཨང་དེབ |
| temperature | *tsha-tsay* | ཚ་ཚད |
| tent | *gur* | གུར |
| test | *tsö-ta* | ཚོད་ལྟ |
| thank | *thug je-chay* | ཐུགས་རྗེ་ཆེ |
| Thank you. | *thug je-chay* | ཐུགས་རྗེ་ཆེ |
| there | *pha-giy* | ཕ་གིར |
| thick | *thugpo* | མཐུག་པོ |
| thief | *kuma* | རྐུ་མ |

| thin | tâbpo | དྭགས་པོ |
| thing | chalag | ཅ་ལག |
| think | sâmlo tongwa | བསམ་བློ་གཏོང་བ |
| thirsty (to be) | kha kompa | ཁ་སྐོམ་པ |
| ticket | pasay/tikasiy | པ་སེ་/ཏི་ཀ་སི |
| time | dü-tsö | དུ་ཚོད |
| tip (gratuity) | ngen-pa/soray | གསོལ་རས་/ཟུར་པ |
| tired (to be) | kâlay kâgpa | དཀའ་ལས་བཀག་པ |
| together | nyâm-du | མཉམ་དུ |
| toilet | sânchö | གསང་སྤྱོད |
| toilet paper | tsâng-dray shugu | གཙང་སྦྲའི་ཤོག་གུ |
| tonight | to-gong | དོ་དགོང |
| too | yâng | ཡང |
| toothbrush | so-trü | སོ་འཁྲུ |
| toothpaste | somen | སོ་སྨན |
| touch (v) | regpa | རེག་པ |
| tour | tâkor | འགྲུ་སྐོར |
| tourist | yukor tochâm-pa | ཡུལ་སྐོར་སྤྲོ་ཚམས་པ |
| toward | chog-la | ཕྱོགས་ལ |
| town | drong-tay | གྲོང་སྡེ |
| track | lâm-shü | ལམ་ཤུལ |
| transit (in) | lâm tshug-la | ལམ་ཚུགས་ལ |
| translate | gyur-wa | སྒྱུར་བ |
| trekking | rilung-la droyak | རི་ལུང་ལ་འགྲོ་ཡག |
| trip | drü-shü | འགྲུལ་བཞུད |
| true | ngö-nay | དངོས་གནས |

| | | |
|---|---|---|
| trust | *lo-kelwa* | བློ་འཁེལ་བ་ |
| try | *bay-pa* | འབད་པ་ |

## U

| | | |
|---|---|---|
| umbrella | *nyi-du* | ཉི་གདུགས་ |
| uncomfortable | *tepo mepa* | བདེ་པོ་མེད་པ་ |
| under | *wog-la* | འོག་ལ་ |
| understand | *ha-go* | ཧ་གོ་ |
| unemployed | *layka maypa* | ལས་ཀ་མེད་པ་ |
| university | *tsug-la lobta* | གཙུག་ལག་སློབ་གྲྭ་ |
| unsafe | *nyen-ga yawpa* | ཉེན་ག་ཡོད་པ་ |
| until | *bar-du* | བར་དུ་ |
| up | *yar* | ཡར་ |
| upstairs | *toga* | ཐོག་ཁ་ |
| use (v) | *bay-chö chay* | བེད་སྤྱོད་བྱེད་ |
| useful | *bay-chö yakpo* | བེད་སྤྱོད་ཡག་པོ་ |

## V

| | | |
|---|---|---|
| vacation | *gung-sâng* | གུང་སངས་ |
| vaccination | *ngön-kok menkâb gyâbpa* | སྔོན་འགོག་སྨན་ཁབ་བརྒྱབ་པ་ |
| valley | *tâng-shong* | ཐང་གཤོང་ |
| valuable | *rin-tâng chenpo* | རིན་ཐང་ཆེན་པོ་ |
| value (price) | *gong* | གོང་ |
| very | *shay-ta* | ཞེ་དྲགས་ |
| view (scenery) | *yü-jong* | ཡུལ་ལྗོངས་ |
| village | *drong-seb* | གྲོང་གསེབ་ |

VOCABULARY

| | | |
|---|---|---|
| visit (v) | *tâkor chay* | དུ་སྐོར་བྱེད་ |
| vomit (v) | *kyug-pa* | སྐྱུག་པ་ |
| vote | *wö-sho lugpa* | འོས་ཤོག་བླུགཔ་ |

## W

| | | |
|---|---|---|
| wait | *gug-pa* | སྒུགཔ་ |
| walk | *gom-pa gyâb* | གོམ་པ་བརྒྱབ་ |
| want | *gaw* | དགོས་ |
|   I want ... | *nga-la ... gaw* | ང་ལ་ ... དགོས། |
|   Do you want ...? | *kayrâng-la ...* *gawpay?* | ཁྱེད་རང་ལ་ ... དགོས་པས། |
| war | *mâg* | དམག |
| warm | *töpo* | དྲོད་པོ་ |
| wash (yourself) | *(sug-po) tru* | ( གཟུགས་པོ་ ) འཁྲུ་ |
| wash (clothes, etc) | *(thug-log) tru* | ( དུག་ལོག་ ) འཁྲུ་ |
| watch (v) | *ta* | བལྟ་ |
| water | *chu* | ཆུ་ |
| water purification tablets | *chu tsâng-ma* *soya-men* | ཆུ་གཙང་མ་བཟོ་ཡག་སྨན་ |
| way | *lâm-ga* | ལམ་ག |
|   Which way? | *lam-ga ka-giy?* | ལམ་ག་ག་གི། |
| wealthy | *gyu-chenpo/choog-po* | རྒྱུ་ཆེན་པོ་/ཕྱུག་པོ་ |
| weather | *nâmshi* | གནམ་གཤིས་ |
| welcome | *tashi delek/kasu-shu* | བཀྲ་ཤིས་བདེ་ལེགས/དགའ་བསུ་ཞུ |
| well | *depo* | བདེ་པོ་ |
| wet | *lönpa* | རློན་པ་ |
| whole | *tshâng-ma* | ཚང་ |

| | | |
|---|---|---|
| wide | *gya-chenpo* | རྒྱ་ཆེན་པོ་ |
| wife | *kyeman* | སྐྱེས་དམན་ |
| win (v) | *tob-pa/gyal-wa* | ཐོབ་པ།/རྒྱལ་བ་ |
| wire | *châg-kü* | ལྕགས་སྐུད་ |
| wise | *kay-pa* | མཁས་པ་ |
| with | *nyâm-du* | མཉམ་དུ་ |
| within | *nâng-la* | ནང་ལ་ |
| without | *chiy-la* | ཕྱི་ལ་ |
| wood | *shing* | ཤིང་ |
| wool | *pay* | བལ་ |
| work | *layka* | ལས་ཀ་ |
| world | *dzâm-ling* | འཛམ་གླིང་ |
| worse | *dug-shö* | སྡུག་ཤོས་ |
| write | *dri-pa* | བྲིས་པ་ |
| wrong | *non-trül* | ནོར་འཁྲུལ་ |

## Y

| | | |
|---|---|---|
| year | *lo* | ལོ་ |
| years ago | *lo mang-pö ngön-la* | ལོ་མང་པོའི་སྔོན་ལ་ |
| yesterday | *kaysâ* | ཁ་སང་ |
| yet | *tânda yâng* | ད་ལྟ་ཡང་ |
| young | *shân-shân* | གཞོན་གཞོན་ |

# Emergencies

| Help! | *rog nâng-da!* | རོགས་པ་གནང་དང༌། |
| Stop!/Wait! | *goo-ro nâng!* | སྒུག་རོགས་གནང༌། |
| Thief! | *kuma du!* | རྐུ་མ། |
| Go away! | *phah gyug!* | ཕར་རྒྱུགས། |
| Watch out! | *mik ta-da* | མིག་བལྟ་དང༌། |
| Fire! | *may ba-giy!* | མེ་འབར་གྱི། |

It's an emergency!
  *dza-drâg ray!*  ཛ་དྲག་རེད།

There's been an accident!
  *phâgay kay-ngen chung sha!*  ཕར་གིར་སྐྱོན་ངན་བྱུང་ཤག

I'll get the police!
  *ngay korsung-wa kay tâng-go!*  ངས་སྐོར་སྲུང་བ་སྐད་གཏོང་གོ

Call a doctor!
  *âmchi kay tong-da!*  ཨེམ་ཆི་སྐད་གཏོང་དང༌།

Call the police!
  *korsung-wa kay tong-da!*  སྐོར་སྲུང་བ་སྐད་གཏོང་དང༌།

Call an ambulance!
  *naypa kye-ken mota kay tong-da!*  ནད་པ་སྐྱེལ་མཁན་མོ་ཊ་སྐད་གཏོང་དང༌།

Could you help me please?
*ku-chi, nga-la rogpa nâng-da*　ཀུ་སྐྱིད། ཉེད་རང་ང་ལ་རོགས་པ་གནང་དང་།

I've been robbed!
*nga kumay chom-song!*　ང་རྐུ་མས་བཅོམ་སོང་།

I've been raped.
*nga-la tsen-wâng-tog chagpa*
*chaysong*　ང་ལ་བཙན་དབང་ཐོག་ཆགས་པ་བྱུང་སོང་།

My ... was stolen.　*ngay ... ku-ma*
*shor-song*　ངའི་ ...... རྐུ་མ་ཤོར་སོང་།

I've lost my ...　*ngay ... lâg-song*　ངའི་ ...... བརླགས་སོང་།

   bags　*bag-la/jola*　འབག་ལག/འཇོ་ལ

   money　*ngü*　དངུལ

   traveller's cheques　*drüshü ngü-dzin*　འགྲུལ་བཞུད་དངུལ་འཛིན

   passport　*chi-thön lâg-teb*　ཕྱིར་ཐོན་ལག་དེབ

I am ill.　*nga nagiy du*　ང་ན་གི་འདུག

I am lost.　*nga lâm-ga lagsha*　ང་ལམ་ཀ་ལག་ཤ

Where is the police station?
*kosung-way le-khung ka-bah*
*yoray?*　སྐོར་སྲུང་བའི་ལས་ཁུངས་ག་པར་ཡོད་རེད།

Where are the toilets?
*sânchö ka-bah yoray?*　གསང་སྤྱོད་ག་པར་ཡོད་རེད།

Could I please use the
telephone?
*kâpa baycho chay-na di-giy*
*rebay?*　ཁ་པར་བེད་སྤྱོད་བྱས་ན་འགྲིག་གི་རེད་པས།

I wish to contact my embassy/
consulate.
*nga shung-tsab-la delwa chay*
*gaw yo*　ང་ཞུང་ཚབ་ལ་འབྲེལ་བ་བྱེད་དགོས་ཡོད།

I don't understand.
   *ngay ha-komasong*                     དས་ཅོ་གོ་གི་མིན་འདུག

I didn't realise I was doing
anything wrong.
   *ngay non-trü chay yawpa*               དས་ནོར་འཁྲུལ་བྱུས་ཡོད་ཅ་ཅོ་མ་སོང་།
   *ha-komasong*

I didn't do it.
   *ngay chay-gyu ma-chung*               དས་བྱེད་རྒྱུ་མ་བྱུང་།

I'm sorry/I apologise.
   *gong-dah*                              དགོངས་དག

Contact number (next of kin)
   *kapa ahng-dâng (pün-nyay*             ཁ་པར་ཨང་གྲངས་(སྤུན་ཉག་ཉི་འོས་)
   *tâg-nyeshö)*

I speak (English).
   *nga (injiy)-kay gya-giy yö*           ང་(དབྱིན་ཇི་)སྐད་རྒྱག་གི་ཡོད།

I have medical insurance.
   *nga-la tröten nyen-sung gaylen*       ང་ལ་འཕྲོད་བསྟེན་ཉེན་སྲུང་བགལ་ལན་
   *shuken yö*                             ཤུགན་ཡོད།

My blood group is (A,B,O,
AB) positive/negative.
   *ngay tra-rig (A,B,O, AB)*             དའི་ཁྲག་རིགས་(ཨེ་བི་འོ་ཨེ་བི་)པོ་/
   *positive/negative*                     ནེ་རེད།

# Index

# LONELY PLANET PHRASEBOOKS

Complete your travel experience with a Lonely Planet phrasebook. Developed for the independent traveller, the phrasebooks enable you to communicate confidently in any practical situation – and get to know the local people and their culture.

Skipping lengthy details on where to get your drycleaning ironed, information in the phrasebooks covers bargaining, customs and protocol, how to address people and introduce yourself, explanations of local ways of telling the time, dealing with bureaucracy and bargaining, plus plenty of ways to share your interests and learn from locals.

Arabic (Egyptian)
Arabic (Moroccan)
Australian
   *Introduction to Australian English,*
   *Aboriginal and Torres Strait languages.*
Baltic States
   *Covers Estonian, Latvian and*
   *Lithuanian.*
Bengali
Brazilian
Burmese
Cantonese
Central Europe
   *Covers Czech, French, German,*
   *Hungarian, Italian and Slovak.*
Eastern Europe
   *Covers Bulgarian, Czech, Hungarian,*
   *Polish, Romanian and Slovak.*
Ethiopian (Amharic)
Fijian
Greek
Hindi/Urdu
Indonesian
Japanese
Korean
Lao
Latin American (Spanish)
Mandarin

Mediterranean Europe
   *Covers Albanian, Greek, Italian,*
   *Macedonian, Maltese, Serbian &*
   *Croatian and Slovene.*
Mongolian
Nepali
Papua New Guinea (Pidgin)
Pilipino
Quechua
Russian
Scandinavian Europe
   *Covers Danish, Finnish, Icelandic,*
   *Norwegian and Swedish.*
Sri Lanka
Swahili
Thai
Thai Hill Tribes
Tibetan
Turkish
USA
   *Introduction to US English,*
   *Vernacular Talk, Native American*
   *languages and Hawaiian.*
Vietnamese
Western Europe
   *Useful words and phrases in Basque,*
   *Catalan, Dutch, French, German, Irish,*
   *Portuguese and Spanish (Castilian).*

# LONELY PLANET AUDIO PACKS

Audio packs are an innovative combination of a cassette/CD and phrasebook presented in an attractive cloth wallet made from indigenous textiles by local communities.

The cassette/CD presents each language in an interactive format. A number of successful language teaching techniques are used, enabling listeners to remember useful words and phrases with little effort and in an enjoyable way.

Travellers will learn essential words and phrases – and their correct pronunciation – by participating in a realistic story. The scripts have been developed in the belief that the best way to learn a new language is to hear it, then to practise it in the context in which you will use it. The emphasis is on effective communication.

The cassette/CD complements the relevant phrasebook, and the cloth wallet makes the pack an attractive and convenient package – easy to display in shops and useful and practical for travellers.

**Cassettes & CDs**
- complement phrasebooks
- realistic storylines explore situations that will be useful for all travellers
- languages are spoken by native speakers
- listeners learn key words and phrases in repetition exercises, then hear them used in context
- realistic sound effects and indigenous music used throughout
- length: 80 minutes

**Cloth Pack**
- ticket-wallet size – suitable for airline tickets, notes etc
- made from traditional textiles woven and sewn by local communities
- cardboard reinforced and sealed in plastic for easy display
- size: 140 x 260 mm

***Available now:*** Indonesian audio pack; Japanese audio pack; Thai audio pack

# PLANET TALK

*Lonely Planet's FREE quarterly newsletter*

Every issue is packed with up-to-date travel news
and advice including:

- a letter from Lonely Planet co-founders Tony and
  Maureen Wheeler
- go behind the scenes on the road with a Lonely
  Planet author
- feature article on an important and topical travel
  issue
- a selection of recent letters from travellers
- details on forthcoming Lonely planet promotions
- complete list of Lonely Planet products

*To join our mailing list contact any Lonely Planet office.*

## LONELY PLANET PUBLICATIONS

**AUSTRALIA**
PO Box 617, Hawthorn 3122, Victoria
tel: (03) 9819 1877  fax: (03) 9819 6459
e-mail: talk2us@lonelyplanet.com.au

**USA**
Embarcadero West,
155 Filbert St, Suite 251,
Oakland, CA 94607
tel: (510) 893 8555
TOLL FREE: 800 275-8555
fax: (510) 893 8563
e-mail: info@lonelyplanet.com

**UK**
10 Barley Mow Passage, Chiswick,
London W4 4PH
tel: (0181) 742 3161  fax: (0181) 742 2772
e-mail: 100413.3551@compuserve.com

**FRANCE**:
71 bis rue du Cardinal Lemoine, 75005
Paris
tel: 1 44 32 06 20  fax: 1 46 34 72 55
e-mail: 100560.415@compuserve.com

**World Wide Web:** http://www.lonelyplanet.com